Based on the Life of
**Linnie Thomas Young**

# Mama Didn't Half-step

## A Mother's Role in Restoring the Family

*Heather DeBerry Stephens*

WESTBOW
PRESS

A DIVISION OF THOMAS NELSON

*WestBow Press books may be ordered through booksellers or by contacting:*

*WestBow Press*
*A Division of Thomas Nelson*
*1663 Liberty Drive*
*Bloomington, IN 47403*
*www.westbowpress.com*
*1-(866) 928-1240*

*Because of the dynamic nature of the Internet, any web addresses or links contained in this book may have changed since publication and may no longer be valid. The views expressed in this work are solely those of the author and do not necessarily reflect the views of the publisher, and the publisher hereby disclaims any responsibility for them.*

*Any people depicted in stock imagery provided by Thinkstock are models, and such images are being used for illustrative purposes only.*

*Certain stock imagery © Thinkstock.*

*ISBN: 978-1-4497-8898-8 (sc)*
*ISBN: 978-1-4497-8899-5 (e)*

*Library of Congress Control Number: 2013905165*

*Printed in the United States of America.*

*WestBow Press rev. date: 04/10/13*

# Dedication

*In memory of*
*Mother Izora Thomas*
*1916-2006*
*"From the seed of a rose!"*

---

*and*
*Helen Woods Payne*
*1944-2007*
*"Beyond thorns lie pedals of beauty."*

# Table of Contents

## "A Recipe for Motherhood"

**The Appetite**

**Preheat the Oven**

**Ingredients: The Introduction**

**Recipe Instructions**

**Ingredients**

# The Appetite

## *Foreword*

I AM BLESSED TO be one of the many who was touched so graciously by Linnie Thomas Young, the subject of this book, "Mama Didn't Half-Step." To know Linnie was an invitation she extended to you to enter into her life. And upon entering, you knew you were in a safe place! Therefore, I was an eyewitness to some of the descriptions of nurturing that are in this book.

Author Heather DeBerry Stephens provides us with a model of a Christian mother, Linnie Thomas Young, who gladly accepted the high calling of motherhood as a priceless gift from God, our Creator. Therefore, Linnie's daily choices, loyalties and allegiances were made in light of her calling as a wife and mother.

Although Heather DeBerry Stephens gives biographical sketches of Linnie's life, she does not ask us to re-invent ourselves into being another Linnie Thomas Young, (this would be superfluous!) Rather, she challenges us, as wives and mothers, to know, trust, and obey the same Savior and Lord, Jesus Christ, who made Himself so visibly known in the life and work of Linnie Thomas Young.

Though mirrored with many challenges to honestly examine ourselves, this book by Heather DeBerry Stephens provides hope for the saving of our families.

**Dr. Erlin Ellena Gooch-Reid**
**Evangelist/Counselor**
**Holly Grove Baptist Church**
**Ripley, Tennessee**

# Preheat the Oven

## *Preface*

WHAT DO WE WISH most for our children? Some might say a better life than we had, meaning prosperity, power and money. Some might desire them to attend a certain college, in order to continue a family tradition. Some parents might want their children to out do the neighbors' children in sports or other activities. There may be some who simply want their children to have a one-way ticket out of their ghettoes, projects, or slums. Some of us may wish for our children to join a certain organization or social group, or maybe to simply live a healthy, happy life. Because of the different economic levels, what one family may view as important may be totally different from another family. Whether you are reading this book representing the lower, middle, or upper class in society, if you believe Jesus to be your personal Savior, then we all should share the same goal for our children—and that desire is salvation.

You know, it's funny how people on the sidelines are always so eager to give their personal opinion of how they would have done things. How they would have hit the winning shot on the basketball court. How they would have chosen different shoes to wear on the red carpet. How they would make better choices when a well-known Fortune 500 company goes under. Worst of all is when they foolishly proclaim how they would never raise their child to behave as some of the negative images that the media portrays today.

Well, this book is not targeting the sideline folks out there pointing fingers and giving opinions. We do not wish to talk about the problems that exist within the family, or criticize others without determining a plan or solution. We wish to be a strong hand lifting each other up. We wish to put our heads together and figure these issues out. On the contrary, the target audience of this book will be people who want change, and are willing to start within themselves to make it happen.

So is it true? Are there really teenagers killing each other over what "hood" they represent or what color they claim? Or what about young girls trying to look and dress sexy in search of affection, only to find molestation, exploitation, rape, prostitution, or death? Is this really happening, or is the media feeding us lies? Is it really true that the average homicide rate for teens ages 15-19 has risen to 9.5% per 100,000? Are we sure about these types of situations? Well guess what? It is true. It is happening in cities and neighborhood like yours and mine. All over the world, as women read this book, many of us will consider our own families with teenagers involved in similar circumstances. Children really are bringing guns to school. They are selling and using drugs and alcohol. They are committing crimes. It's no secret. We all know. The question is what do we do to fix this problem? If the children really are our future, like the song goes, how promising does our future presume to be?

Well, before you can change something you must first identify exactly what it is you want to adjust. Now, we can definitely say that the American family, particularly our youth, is in trouble. The characteristics of a dysfunctional family are becoming more acceptable as normal. Whether the problem directly or indirectly affects you, the future of our children is at stake. The first question is, "How did we get here?" If *we* can avoid doing what has brought us to this point, then maybe <u>we</u>, as a universal family can obtain different and better results.

Let's go back to the word "we." So who does "we" refer to? Well, since God chose to make me a female, I would like to speak directly to the women, or should I say the mothers of the world. Even if you have not physically given birth, you still have a responsibility to exercise the natural maternal instincts that are divinely embedded within. Oh yes, the mothers—those who walked around with the big stomachs, big noses, big breasts, and especially the big appetites for forty weeks. The ones who bore the labor, survived the delivery, and endured the emotional roller coasters, and sleepless nights for days and weeks to come. To the women who have accepted the Most High's calling of motherhood, to raise the world's children as unto the Lord. To the mothers whose purpose in life is to develop law abiding, respectful, disciplined, and fun-loving children that will grow up to be successful and productive members of the human race. Women, I'm speaking to you!

The old saying goes, "the hand that rocks the cradle is the hand that rules the world". In most cases, that hand is the hand of a mother. The one who kisses the child's bruise when he falls, making the pain magically go away. There is power in the hand of a mother. Power to strike that child with the rod of loving discipline. Power to rub those sick children with alcohol (ointment) until the fever breaks and they fall fast asleep. So, it does not seem unreasonable to say that a mother can play a significant role in restoring the family.

So mothers, what happened? What went wrong?

Let's go to the couch, sit down and grab the remote. Go ahead and turn on the news. What was that we were saying earlier, "*...if it were my child...*", "*I wish I would find my child doing such a thing.*" We can always criticize what others have done, but what are we doing? Well, to all the sideline mothers talking about what you would have done and what they should have done, I say to you, *we* have dropped the figurative ball of parenting. In simpler terms, we have ***half-stepped.*** I'm sure we all know what the word "half-step" means. In case you don't know what it means, why don't I just break it down for you?

Imagine being at your favorite college's homecoming football game. Imagine the excitement in the air— the smell of the popcorn, the crowd, the cheerleaders, the whole nine yards. Oh, how you love to be entertained by the dynamic performance of the marching band during the half-time show. We all know the tall, skinny drum major, complete with his hat and baton. He will lead the band onto the field with a sharp, high-stepping strut—never a sloppy half-step. His march sets the tone of pride and commitment to their craft as musicians and entertainers. Each member of the band will follow the drum major, marching with the same level of precision. Unfortunately, in the band of motherhood, our marching style leaves much room for improvement. There's much more to be desired.

Many of us are half-stepping on our jobs as mothers, and we need to admit it.

So, I'd like to get the attention of every mother, mama, mommy, big mama, madea, or whatever you answer to. I'm calling a meeting in the ladies room. That's right! It's time for us to huddle in a circle, stand in the gap—do something! We must talk this thing out. The time is crucial for us to determine how to refrain from the half-stepping that has brought our families to this point of disappointment, sadness and hurt.

Ladies, we must realize that this sad reality that exists today is not what God wants for us. Do you honestly believe Jesus came and gave his life for this?

**"I have come that they may have life, and that they may have it more abundantly." John 10:10**

Life, abundant life. Is abundant life drug abuse? Is abundant life anorexia? Is abundant life depression leading to suicide? Whoa, the heaviness of this situation is unbearable.

Now, don't get me wrong, mothers. I'm not blaming this problem entirely on us. The old proverb, *"It takes a village to raise a child,"* still holds true. In addition, the enemy—Satan, uses many channels to constantly try to throw us off our A-game. His job is to kill, steal, and destroy, by any means necessary. Satan wants to see us all half-step, and that includes mothers, fathers, family members, neighbors, teachers and friends. Yes, the responsibility lies in the hands of many. Yet, in this book, I'd like to address the mother's role in restoring the family.

Mothers must understand that it will truly require a 100% effort to put us back on the right track. Some mothers just don't know any better. They simply give that which was given to them. Nonetheless, we cannot continue to believe our half-stepping efforts are enough. Now, if anyone in the family should be "on point" or should I say on top of her job, it should be the mother. Even though there are several others who play a role in raising our children, it does not negate the fact that a mother's involvement in the life of a child is fundamental for their healthy emotional, mental, and spiritual development.

To knock down a wall, every person must push with 100%, complete, absolute, total force. If each person gives less than a full push, the wall won't budge. However, if each person gives 100% effort, with faith in God's power, mountains can be moved.

So, as we agree on the problem at hand, we recognize the need to make a bad situation better. The key rule here is, just don't half-step. In its simplest terms, just don't half-step. In layman's terms, just don't half-step. Whether in encouragement or in chastisement, don't half-step. In support or attention, don't half-step. In conversation or quality time, don't half-step. In love or in discipline, just don't half-step. Whenever you extend your hand in the life of that child, no matter what, don't half-step!

Some may say this is easier said than done. Can a mother really give 100% effort in all that she does for her children? Is there anyone out there who can say his or her mother did not half-step? If so, we want to know how she did it. Maybe we need an example, an operations manual to turn to, or a technical support help desk to call. Is there anyone out there who can tell us how to stop half-stepping and become the mothers we were born to be?

We know that only Jesus was perfect, and none of us will ever be. God knew we needed a role model and He sent Jesus to be a perfect example for us. Even Dora the Explorer teaches our young children, *"When you don't know which way to go, turn to the map."* If only there was someone who had it together, and did not half-step as a mother. If only we mothers had a real example. Well, ladies and gentlemen, boys and girls, young and old, the moment is at hand. It is now time for the world to meet a mother who made the choice not to half-step. Allow me to bless you with the spirit, the life, the legacy, and the love of none other than ....... **Sister Linnie Thomas Young**.

Yes, my friends, Sister Young, as she was mostly

called, gave 100% to all of her children and never skipped a beat. In every way that each of her children needed her, Sister Young came full force and never half-stepped. So is this, "Project Don't Half-Step" achievable? The answer is yes. Sister Young did it, and so can we. Many mothers give the lame excuse, *"I did all I knew to do,"* but was that really true? When we learn better, it is our responsibility to do better. Sister Young was able to truly do her very best as a mother because of her obedience to God. When we are not completely living our lives for God, it stunts our growth in so many other areas of our lives. Due to our selfishness, it's impossible to be the women of God that we are all called to be.

Growing higher and higher in Christ was Sister Young's first priority. In order for one to achieve this, one must regularly pray, fast, study, hear, and speak God's word. The key word in that statement is regularly-meaning daily, all the time, often, a way of life. To the average person, that seems like too much pressure. *"What about me? What about my hobbies? What about my self-indulgent pleasures? Today's my day off, so I must catch up on my favorite TV shows, gossip on the phone with my girlfriends, chat on Facebook for hours, and then I must go shopping. Let's not forget my hair and nail appointment. I just don't have time to spend with God."* This may sound silly, but the reality is until we deny ourselves, feed our spirit, and live each day like it was our last opportunity to impress positivity upon our children, then the problem that our children now face will only worsen.

I'm not at all saying that to be a good mother you cannot enjoy life. Sister Young laughed all the time. She was always smiling and happy. She lived a Christian life, but she always kept it real. She had an excellent way of balancing her spirituality with every day life. The key is…

> *"Seek ye first the Kingdom of God and His righteousness, and all these things will be added unto you." –Matthew 6:33*

Sister Young brought these words to life—words we should all live by. She was a true disciple of God, and through His divine direction, she was able to be a positive influence on her children and so many others.

In this book, we will address areas where mothers today are half-stepping. A great number of problems could have possibly been avoided if Mama had not half-stepped. This book will also offer a number of solutions to this harsh reality, while we examine some of Sister Young's approaches that may influence some new parenting practices of our own.

Sister Young's life was like a dictionary for the

mis-speller, like orientation for the new-hire. Her life was a good, positive, and above all, Christian example of how to live. More specifically, she showed us that being happy and a good mother are both achievable. Although her love stretched wider, stronger and deeper than motherhood alone, Sister Young was an exceptional mother and was sent to be an example for us.

Yes, many of our families are in trouble. We must, therefore, read this book with an open heart. During the course of reading this book, take this very moment to examine yourself. Never think about someone else's situation without also examining your own. This may be tough, but it is certainly needed in order to mend that which is broken. In our own private time, we should take this as an opportunity to make sure we are not half-stepping as mothers. Let this book not be another form of gossip or criticism toward our neighbor. Rather, let this be a time of re-examining and renewing our purpose. Some things can be easily fixed, if we just humble ourselves enough to identify the problem and admit it exists. Just like the elderly lady in the commercial, "we've fallen" but it's time to get up. Mothers of the world, it's time to get up. Let us join hands and unite. United we stand!

# Ingredients: The Introduction

## Ode to Sister Young

*Being around her was warm.*
*Warm, can anyone relate to that?*
*Linnie Young was a woman who led in the laughter,*
*known commonly to exhort, uplift, and encourage.*
*Her warmth overflowed.*
*Her love blessed your soul.*
*She brought out your best.*
*Thank God for Sister Young.*

"SISTER" —NOW LET'S EXPLORE that word. This term, commonly used in the church, is a proper or formal title to a woman's name, much like Aunt Donna or Uncle Chris. Well, in describing Sister Young, she was a sister and so much more. Some describe her spirit as that of an angel. If you were around her, even for a brief moment, you were either touched in some way by her spirit, or she directly led you to the Lord. Yes, she was warm, simply because she made you feel warm inside. God's love was felt so heavily through Sister Young, and there is still so much that her legacy has to share with us all.

> *" If I am lifted up from the earth, I'll draw all men unto me." John 12:32*

Now, let's get it straight on the front end. Celebrating the legacy of Sister Young is not intended to be any type of cult-like ploy to worship her in any way. I rebuke the enemy's tricks with that. What I would like to celebrate is her commitment to obey and allow God to show Himself through her good works. It is refreshing to know that someone got this motherhood task right.

As we look at what God can truly do in our lives, we can see for ourselves what He has in store, if we only have faith and obey. Through obedience to His Word, we can find the solutions to restoring the lives of our children. Through obedience to His Word, we can learn to be women who step high in our roles as mothers. We will have children who bring us joy and not sorrow. We will let God show us a higher level of happiness through our children. Beyond that, consider every other positive and wonderful experience to be icing on the cake. We will become virtuous women of God who will make a strong effort not to half-step. Real talk—that's what this book is all about.

It's so amazing, simply incredible the way God sends one of his own to do a specific work, at a specific time, for a specific purpose. Indeed, Sister Young was sent to love. Although her love stretched wider and deeper than motherhood alone, she was sent to be an example to many. You know what? Let's just slow it down and learn a little more about Sister Young.

# As a Child

OKAY, ARE WE READY to ride the wave of the life of a real mother? Well, it all began March 7, 1940 in Memphis, Tennessee, where Linnie was born the daughter of Izora and Odell Thomas. As a child, she was set apart from the start. Izora, or Mother Thomas as she was called by many, remembered Linnie to be a very obedient child who loved to learn. Mother Thomas explained, *"Linnie was never a worrisome, or should I say a rebellious child. She accepted the word 'no'."*

The Thomas family came from very humble beginnings, and there was little money for toys and extra luxuries most families enjoy today. One day, as the family enjoyed an evening sitting on the porch, Mother Thomas noticed something that instantly warmed her heart. She saw little Linnie sitting with her legs hanging on the inside of the steps, pretending the step above her was her piano. She passionately enjoyed singing and playing her pretend piano. This touched Mother Thomas so deeply that she vowed to save her pennies to purchase a piano for her daughter, if it was the last thing she did. When God blessed them with a piano, it was off to Mrs. Netherwood's house, the local piano teacher, and, of course, Linnie was quick to learn. She would practice for hours, everyday. There was a time when her father would beg her to please give it a rest. Little did they know that the piano would be such an important instrument in Linnie's life.

As early as her teenage years, she was already using her musical gift by playing for a prominent minister in the Memphis area. The piano later became her tool for glorifying God, as she directed choirs and led in worship services. Thank God Mother Thomas paid attention to her child playing her pretend piano on the steps that day. We, as mothers, should also cultivate the natural interests of our children, while they are young.

Linnie's brother, Henry, remembered her to be very competitive. He called her a good winner and a good loser. He was proud to speak about how close he and his sister were, as children and as adults. Henry had fond memories of how he would lie across the foot of her bed and they would talk for hours. He explained, *"With Linnie, nothing was too bad, too good, or too personal. She was a real friend."*

Linnie was a natural leader. She loved to teach and help her friends in the neighborhood. She was also feisty, now. She feared no bullies, and they didn't mess with her either. She didn't start fights, but she definitely defused them with her "no nonsense" demeanor.

Linnie also enjoyed learning about God. It's no surprise that she accepted Jesus Christ at a young age, around 10 or 11, as Mother Thomas remembered. Even her teachers would often comment on her winning personality. There was one occasion that Mother Thomas remembered a slight attitude from her daughter. She asked Linnie, *"Where's my smile?"* and of course, she lost the attitude and gave her mother a smile.

Linnie was popular in high school. As a matter of fact, she once used her popularity to help out a good friend. There was a boy who wasn't really attractive, and was often talked about and teased. So, Linnie decided to pretend to date him just so he could gain acceptance among his peers. Well, her little plan worked, and he soon became "one of the guys". This young man always held high regards for Linnie Thomas. That young man happened to be none other than the legendary Isaac Hayes.

After graduating salutatorian from Manassas High School, Linnie's mind was set for college. During the

1960's, the opportunities for African-Americans were more challenging, but to Linnie, the sky was the limit. She packed her bags, and in 1958 headed for Tuskegee Institute in Alabama (now Tuskegee University).

# As a Young Lady

Do you think a woman of Linnie's caliber would choose a simple course of study? (I didn't think so, either.) She chose to study in Chemistry, and boy, did she study! In fact, she excelled to the point of Summa Cum Laude. Her level of leadership led her to join Delta Sigma Theta Sorority, Incorporated. In addition to being named Ms. Delta, Linnie was inducted into "Who's Who Among American Colleges and Universities." She participated in student government and was named Homecoming Queen. The list goes on and on, yet she was always very modest and never bragged about her accomplishments.

> **"...not to think of himself more highly than he ought to think, but to think soberly, as God has dealt to each one a measure of faith."** *Romans 12:3*

Linnie's college life was very fulfilling. She wasn't the type of person to go away to school and get wild. She had an excellent college experience. She participated in many organizations and accomplished much. She pledged, she partied, and she loved to dance. She did her thing. Yet, Linnie maintained her dignity as she grew into womanhood while away at school. She shared her experiences with her family back home, especially her brother Henry, who was away in the service. He lived his own "college experiences" vicariously through the letters she would write to him. Although one of her professors nicknamed her "Ole Baptist Linnie", she balanced her spiritual lifestyle with secular activities without compromising her values.

**" I say then: walk in the spirit, and you shall not fulfill the lust of the flesh." *Galatians 5:16***

After four years of college, Linnie proudly prepared for the glorious occasion of graduation. She had this big plan to strut her stuff across the stage on graduation day. You know, the world today teaches us that it's good to brag and boast. This is the "bling-bling" era, and everyone wants to self-indulge. Both rich and poor go through hundreds, and for some thousands of dollars on our hair, nails, Botox, reconstructive surgeries, tanning beds... oh, I could go on and on naming our acts of vanity. I haven't even mentioned our clothes, our rides, and our jewelry. So for Linnie to fantasize about having a *"Yeah, I did it"* walk across the stage, it would appear that even she had a little vanity down deep within. Well, when the time came, she unexpectedly felt the glory of God's presence upon her. Instead of strutting her stuff across the stage, she could only sing along as the choir performed the old Negro Spiritual, *"I Know He Laid His Hand On Me."* At that moment, she was lifted to a higher level in God. Hallelujah!

**"Happy is the man who finds wisdom, and the man who gains understanding"** *Proverbs 3:13*

# As a Wife

AFTER COLLEGE, LINNIE MOVED back to her hometown of Memphis, TN. Eager to begin her career, she was hired by Buckman Laboratories on July 9, 1962. As the story goes, Linnie was said to have made history by becoming the first African-American, Level-1 Chemist in Memphis. This legend was not officially verified, however, it was those who lived in Memphis during that time who began this remarkable rumor. She certainly had all qualifications for a promising career to secure her financially.

Everything in her life was going well so far, but it only got better. Later that year, she met....... **Mr. Ben Young**. Ben Young was a bit older and far more "worldly" experienced than Linnie, but as they say, opposites attract. He saw something in her, and she in him. The two began to spend more time together. Soon, Ben started going to church to win Linnie's approval. He didn't know what an effect this pretty lady would have on him in changing the course of his destiny.

They were truly friends first. Besides, we already know that only a friend would try to help make you a better person. Friends do things like influence you to stop smoking, lead you to Christ—you know, things like that, right? That's just what Linnie did for Ben. Because of his strong interest in becoming closer to Linnie, Ben welcomed the changes that she influenced in his life.

Now, in Mother Thomas' opinion, Ben was not exactly the perfect choice for her daughter. At that time, Ben was heavy with the ladies, and ever heavier with the liquor. Oh, but Linnie saw so much more. After a three year courtship, the two were married on June 26, 1965.

Linnie Thomas Young was the type of woman who saw the real potential in her husband. Women like this desire to see their husband be the man of God they are intended to be. If you hear me ladies, you can relate to Sister Young. She had a remarkable gift of encouraging Brother Ben to greater heights, without threatening his manhood or integrity.

The children remember very few arguments between their parents. Sister Young truly respected her husband, and never asserted authority over him—rather; she exhorted him and supported him. Not to say there were never frustrations present within their marriage, because there were. However, the beauty of it was that Sister Young's humble, submissive spirit never caused her to forget her God-given role and purpose. Yes, she was more educated than Brother Ben. Yes, she was more exposed and polished and articulate. She had many qualities that could have made her arrogant, and would have probably created resentment and jealously from her husband. Sister Young, however, understood her role. She was his wife and not his competitor. She delighted in seeing Brother Ben grow to become a great man of God. Even as a wife, she did not half-step.

With her prayers and God's grace, Brother Ben blossomed. Mother Thomas said, *"Ben became a church going man."* He began to study the bible and just couldn't stop. He would study and study, stop and pray, then meditate and study some more. As time went on, he lived to become a great spiritual leader and man of God. He started with a small ministry in the family center of Lamar Terrace Housing Projects. From there, he was appointed to pastor a small church by the Southern Baptist Association, and later an even bigger church. He became the first African-American pastor for the Shelby Baptist Association of the Southern Baptist Convention. He later went on to become the first African -American President of the Preachers School at Union University. All of these great things were what God allowed Sister Young to foresee in the very beginning.

It was Sister Young's purpose to be a true help-meet for her husband. Yes, she kept the house and raised the children, but a true helper meant assisting with the fulfillment of her husband's destiny. Brother Ben was destined to be a great leader of God's people. Sister Young's support helped Brother Ben carry out this spiritual assignment. Sister Young did far more than just sit in the "Amen corner", wearing a pretty hat. Her role as First Lady meant serving as a Sunday School Teacher, Minister of Music, pianist, evangelism team leader, Women's Ministry Leader, Vacation Bible School Director, Youth Director, bus driver, and church custodian. I'm sure I probably missed something, but these were ways, in which, she definitely helped Brother Ben carry out his ministry.

**"Wives, submit to your own husbands, as to the Lord."** *Ephesians 5:22*

Even though Sister Young was active in so many areas, she had the unique gift of always allowing Brother Ben to feel like a leader. Her admiration for him was always present and heavily felt, as she served in her various capacities in the church and in his life. When Brother Ben would say certain outlandish things in some of his sermons, Sister Young would always give a certain smile that everyone could relate to. She never showed signs of embarrassment or resentment on behalf of her husband. All the while, Sister Young was still the unsung hero who was loved by everyone.

# As a Friend

ONE OF THE FIRST descriptions of Sister Young, from someone who cherished her as a friend, was that she was in tune with and respected God's direction. His direction led her to glorify Him in all that she did. She was also very humble. Sister Young never cared who got the credit, as long as God got the glory. What saddened her, however, were things that would displease God. You see, Sister Young talked the talk, but through her devotion to God, she also walked the walk. She was not the type to ever be on the "down low" with anything. She kept it real.

What amazed me was when her close friend, with whom she had many long conversations, reported that she never, ever heard Sister Young gossip. What? How is that humanly possible? Our world is based on gossip. Our TV is based on gossip. Our music is based on gossip. If you think about it, movies are nothing but an entire storyline of us viewing into the lives of the characters, thus creating something for the world to gossip about. We will sit through a two-hour movie, just to be the spectator watching the highs and lows of the characters' lives. Why? So we can get all up in their business and be nosey and gossip. It's what we love. It's what we thirst. We use gossip for advertisement and publicity. From gossip columns to gossip magazines, in today's world, gossip is money and power. Nonetheless, Sister Young didn't even gossip when she prayed. She was confidential. She was a true friend.

There wasn't much that anyone could say negatively about Sister Young. She was just a joy to be around. Everyone loved her energy, as she was full of life. As a friend, she never judged you. She didn't make you feel bad if your lifestyle wasn't squeaky clean. Moreover, she gained your respect to make you want to do better. You didn't want to curse or drink or any of that around her, because she represented goodness. Everyone respected her walk because it was real.

There was an incident once when she was on a trip that truly exemplified Sister Young's character. While on this trip, she met a man who tried to flirt with her. She didn't "dis" him or offend him. All she did was maintain her personal integrity. By the end of the trip, he too had obviously developed a level of respect for Sister Young, because he thanked her for being who she was—a holy woman of God!

**"...because it is written, 'Be holy,
for I am holy.'"** *I Peter 1:16*

It was so pleasing to hear that Sister Young's selfless deeds had not gone unrecognized. All of her closest friends and relatives planned a Love Day Celebration in honor of Sister Young. It was on this day that those who had been touched by this great woman of God could express their sincerest appreciation for all that she had been in their lives. During the Love Day Celebration, many people were able to show their appreciation for the many years Sister Young offered herself as someone they could turn to for advice, council, friendship, favors, and especially love. This day was probably long overdue.

Now on that night, Sister Young was feeling ill due to her cancer diagnosis (which we will discuss, in length, later in the book) and almost opted out of attending the appreciation. After much prodding and pleading from her children, she finally conjured up enough strength and pushed out to attend what she thought was a regular church service. It was just like Sister Young to press on, in spite of how she felt, even though she had no idea that the surprise event was for her.

There was singing and tributes to warm her heart. As a grand finale, Sister Young was given a robe and a crown was placed upon her head by her eldest son. With a humble spirit, Sister Young thanked them all for their thoughtfulness. She recognized all those who had worked so hard to prepare such an event. Yet, she deemed herself unworthy of the crown and robe. In humility, she took off the crown and robe, and as she laid them down she proclaimed that she would rather lay them upon the feet of our Father. She spoke of her hopes for a heavenly crown, as there was yet work to be done.

**"...for when he has been approved, he will receive the crown of life which the Lord has promised to those who love Him."** *James 1:12*

Sister Young had lots of friends, and she poured into their lives through kindness. She was of strong moral support to many pastors' wives. She was an advisor for many local conferences and retreats. Throughout the city, many churches would call upon her to render her musical gift of singing and playing the piano. (By the way, she never charged a fee.) To sum it up, Sister Young was a jewel of a friend.

# As a Mother

AFTER BEING MARRIED JUST a few years, Sister Young wanted to embark on the beauty and joy of motherhood. Her very first pregnancy went full-term, but ended in a still-birth. That, however, did not discourage Sister Young from trying again. In 1966, Sister Young became pregnant with another child, who would be proudly known as her first child, Joy Demetria. This fitting name was certainly what she felt—overflowing joy.

**"The babe leapt in my womb for joy."** *Luke 1:44*

Joy was born on February 21, 1967. Sister Young continued to work as a chemist at Buckman Laboratories, while taking care of her sweet daughter and family. When she became pregnant with baby number two, the "working Mom" thing did not appear to be how she wanted to devote her time. She could no longer deny God's calling on her life. There was no salary that a job could pay that was worth distracting Sister Young from parenting, for she understood and accepted her assignment as a mother. She walked away from this "good job" and became a full time care-giver for her beautiful daughter Joy and her unborn child. On January 15, 1969, baby Steven Benard (named after his father, Ben) was born. The happy mother was free from all career ties and was happy to be a full-time wife and mother of two.

Oh, the perfect family—Mom, Dad, baby girl and baby boy. The size of their family seemed feasible to make ends meet with only one income. They had it all. Well, not quite. You see, God granted favor upon Linnie to be a mother. So He allowed her to show and prove His glory. God gave them one more child on June 9, 1970, another baby boy, Kevin Henry (named after her brother, Henry).

Now they had three children, one income, and God's grace. Do you think they stopped with three children? How about another three on top of that? On January 13, 1972 was born another son, Corey Thomas (given her maiden name, Thomas). Then, a daughter was born on July 21, 1973, Kia Linnette (her namesake, Linnie). Finally, little "Peanut", Camille Izora-DeAnn (named after Linnie's mother Izora and her dear friend, Deanna Goosby) was born on June 30, 1975.

What do you think was produced from a home of six children and two parents on one income? The answer was a whole lot of fun, laughs, memories, and much love. The children remember days that their stomachs hurt from hours of laughter. They all had so much fun together.

In today's society, we would call having six children on one lower-middle class income foolish, chaotic, and irresponsible. Oh, but when you walk in the will of God, He will make the impossible become effortless.

**"I can do all things through Christ, which strengthens me."** *Philippians 4:13*

There's no denying that Sister Young was ordained to be a mother. She was so phenomenal that she even took in an exchange student from Zimbabwe, Africa. Can you believe that? I'm sure many of us would have shaken her and said, *"Linnie, six children already and you're gonna take in another child? Really?"* Not to mention, the many sleepovers, after school, and over-night care that, many times, resulted in a multitude of children being in the house, at one time. The average woman would not even have considered such a thing, but Sister Young was certainly not your average woman.

Sister Young not only gave tirelessly of herself to her family, but she was a constant giver to people in general. She was a listener. She would make you feel as though your problem was the most important thing in the world at that particular moment. She would give all that she had to people, whether it was money, food, time, prayers, or Godly advice. One day, someone admired her coat that she was wearing and she literally gave that woman the "coat off her back." You name it, she made it happen. Her children remembered how people would constantly call the house to speak with their mother for advice and counsel. They never remembered their mother to complain.

There was just something special about Sister Young. I suppose it's called the, "It Factor" today. She certainly had "it." This is why she was so highly loved and respected. I have come across people who only knew her briefly, and even they would strongly comment on how nice or sweet she was. Do we leave that impression on everyone we encounter? Probably not, since we live our lives with such selfish philosophies as "Me, myself and I," "It's all about me," or "Get yours because I'm gonna get mine." Society teaches us to consider ourselves first, but the Word of God teaches us to consider our neighbor before ourselves. Sister Young's mentality was different from our modern-day thinking. Which mentality do you think pleases God?

We will explore in greater detail examples of how Sister Young interacted in the lives of her children. Generally speaking, she was the type mother who made time for her children by supporting the areas of their needs, and their desires in life. She took time to teach vital life lessons. She was heavily involved at each of her children's schools. As a matter fact, she was the Memphis City Schools Parent Teacher Association (PTA, now called the Parent Teacher Organization, PTO) President, and she inspired many parents, both mothers and fathers, to give of themselves as she did. Yes, she kept her children busy, but not with the intent of keeping them out of her hair. She was busy right along with them. She taught them how to use their time productively.

Motherhood was only a piece of the puzzle as it relates to Sister Young's accomplishments. The memory of Sister Young will continue to touch our hearts, and those of our children's children. We recognize the life of this extraordinary woman to be a positive example. She was a godly, humble shepherd who never stopped striving. Yet, of all her talents and gifts, the greatest gift to her and of her was motherhood.

# Recipe Instructions

WHY DO SOME MOTHERS live their lives as if tomorrow is actually promised? We all know that old saying, "Here today, gone tomorrow." Considering the rise of fatal sicknesses and diseases, accidental deaths and natural disasters, one would think it to be clear that every day should be savored. We hear about shootings and killings every night on the news. Yet, why is it that some mothers feel as though they have all the time in the world guaranteed to be a good mother?

These are expressions of the many excuses that mothers give for not properly parenting their child(ren): *Oh, I'm working too much right now; I don't have time to take my children anywhere fun; I'll get around to it later; No, I don't let my kids play sport because I can't be tied up taking them to and from practice; I don't have time to really talk to my daughter about the pressures from boys, or my son about bad influences; I know they are my responsibility, but I'm too preoccupied with so many other things; I'll just have to leave that in the hands of their immature friends, and their uncaring teachers for now; Hopefully, everything will turn out ok.*

A mother who half-steps in the area of spending time with her child(ren) is a mother who likes to gamble. This is just like playing Russian Roulette with your child. That may sound strange, but a gambler takes chances/risks, that carry high stakes. There is a chance you might win, and a chance you might lose. When your children are in the company of anyone other than yourself, there is a possibility or risk that your children may learn bad/poor habits. There is also a risk of them being hurt or abused. Now, what real mother really wants to risk anything that relates to her children? I would like to think none of us; yet, we continue to allow other things to take precedence over spending quality time with our own children. If everything else is more important than being with your child, then you face the risk of leaving them in situations that may not be safe or suitable. No, you cannot be with your children 100% of the time. However, the quality time that you do spend with them will make a lasting impression. The key term here is "quality" time. If you do not invest your time in them, then someone else will. You are foolishly taking a gamble with the influences your child will encounter, thus illustrating the fact that you are gambling with your child's short and long-term well-being.

Well, someone might say, "*I don't let my child hang out.*" That may be true, but there are ways that our children are exposed to negativity right in our very homes. If you don't want your child cursing, then why do you expose them to music with explicit lyrics and/or use those words around them? If you don't want your child fascinated with guns and killing, then why don't you restrict their movies and video games? Believe me, the world will expose them to these things every chance imaginable. However, if you are spending designated quality time with your child, it is then that you can talk about these things and help your child understand why those negative influences are wrong. Who else is going to tell your child the truth? The enemy wants to feed your child lies, but it is your job to continually fight against the world's influences on your child's mind.

Let's explore some of the reasons we are too busy to spend time with our children. Some reasons may be out of our control. However, these are simply obstacles that must be worked through. For example, one reason that quickly comes to mind is the fact that many mothers work outside the home. They have no other means for providing for the family, because Daddy is not doing his part—whether they are still in a relationship of some sort with the mother or not. Unfortunately, for many single mothers, working is mandatory for survival. This brings me to the question, *"Fathers, where are you? Why aren't you here? We desperately need you!!!"*

Let's stop a minute and look at this. Now, if all fathers were in place, pulling your own weight, with no excuses, with your boots laced tight, facing all odds, all obstacles, all restrictions that many men face, doing whatever it takes to provide, lead, and protect your family, then what difference do you think it would make in the success of the family? One difference would be that Mama could place more time and focus on home and the children. All that we are about to discuss in each of these chapters would be more attainable if fathers would step up. This was how Sister Young was able to be all that she was. Her husband did not expect her to be an outstanding mother and wife, and work a demanding job, too. I'm not saying it is not possible, but for mothers working outside the home, it would definitely make it be more challenging. After saying all that, I feel a need to stop and intercede for our fathers for a brief moment.

*Prayer: Father God, in the name of Jesus, we pray for our fathers. We pray that your Holy Spirit convicts their hearts to be the mighty men of God that they were created to be. First, lead them to have a mind to truly submit their lives to You. Show husbands how to truly love their wives and their children, as Christ loved the church and gave His life for it. Oh Lord, teach them how to truly trust You to equip them to take care of their families. If You get our families back into Your divine order, there will be nothing preventing us from doing our parts as mothers. Our families and lives will be blessed. Only You can make this happen. So we lift up all fathers of the world, in Jesus name. Amen.*

Well, I'm sure the enemy has led many fathers astray. It's the enemy's strategic ploy to destroy the family, starting with the "head." Many fathers have come to believe that the "selfish" mothers of their children would not appreciate them doing more to support their children, especially financially, so why bother? These mothers may take advantage of the father's generosity and misuse the money. There are also fathers who want to be in the children's lives but the mothers won't allow them to. Whatever the obstacle may be, there is still no excuse for fathers to neglect raising and providing for their own children. Nonetheless, there are a lot of women who still would not be better mothers, even if they had the full support and participation of the biological father. This is why there is such a need for mothers to use this book to place our priorities in the proper perspective. So let's return our focus back on our mothers.

Another reason that mothers today half-step in their roles is because they have not truly submitted their hearts to God. When you don't have the Holy Spirit dwelling within you, to lead and guide your actions, your tongue and your heart, then all types of evils may take control. Many mothers simply don't know any better. This is why it is important that we, as believers, exercise every opportunity to let our Godly light shine. His light will shine brightly through each of us, just as it did through Sister Young, if we submit to God's will and way.

We have let the ways of the world dominate the truth of God. We, the church of today, should be ashamed. I'm talking about the "church folks" who fill the pews every Sunday with their shouts of praise, yet they live as the minority, in fear of being the bold disciples of Christ that we are supposed to be. I'm asking you to think about our leaders, our pastors, our politicians, living in fear of actually practicing what they preach. "Things have to be politically correct," says the system we have conditioned our lives to. So instead of speaking the truth, living the truth, and raising our children under the truth, we go as far as consenting to have Santa Claus and Easter bunnies right in the church. So, shame...shame on us all!

The Bible teaches us that the older women are supposed to teach the younger women the way to love their "own" husband and their children. So why is it that those women with knowledge and wisdom of the truth seem afraid to share it? Instead, they so often take the *"It's not my business,"* approach. Well, guess what, if you care about the direction that our world is going in, understand that it is your business. Every time you see another mother mistreat or neglect her child, will you pray for the right words and offer them to that mother? What if your simple words of wisdom become a revelation in the life of that mother and child? Sometimes, the greatest revelation for some people is not even found in words. It's sometimes found through being an example. Sister Young was bold in her conversations and wise in her teaching. Best of all, she lived out and exemplified her ministry of motherhood. As Sister Young did, we too must have courage, we must take responsibility, and we must make a difference.

**"...that they admonish the young women to love their husbands, to love their children, to be discrete, chaste, homemakers, good and obedient to their own husbands, that the word of God may not be blasphemed." *Titus 2:4-5***

Another reason mothers don't invest their time and energy into their children is because many mothers are not mature. Although maturity is not always defined by age, it is sad that so many teenagers are having children. Many young mothers will admit that they wanted someone to love them, so they became pregnant as a means of creating a source of the love they desire to receive. Under these circumstances, where was that teenager's mother? If there was a void in the teenager's life, perhaps her own mother could have done a better job of filling that emptiness. A mother's influence can lead a young girl toward a larger desire to achieve more than premarital pregnancy. A mother's love builds self-worth. When a mother shares the love of God with her daughter, she shows her that she is an heir to His throne, and that she was fearfully and wonderfully made. On the contrary, the void of this love will send a young girl searching for it. So, when that boy whispers in her ear, she becomes an easy target. Searching for love, she finds all the wrong things. As she journeys that path, she is susceptible to find a ruined reputation, pregnancy, disease, abuse, and even death.

Why do you think teen pregnancy is so common? It is evident that spiritual warfare heavily exists in this area. First of all, the world uses seduction to sell music, to increase movie revenue, and really to do most everything, in terms of advertising and marketing. Seduction is glorified and emphasized.

It's the subject of many secular songs, and we all know how much music influences our children. We already know what we are up against when raising our daughters to embrace purity. So mothers, how have you really equipped your daughters? Have you schooled her on what those little boys in her ear really want? Have you told her how precious her virginity is? What about protecting her reputation? Forget all that. Is she familiar with the word "fornication?" No one wants to speak the truth anymore. Instead of emphasizing being "safe," why don't we promote abstinence? Let's be real. The teachings of the world are so backwards, and we just follow along, too afraid to question anything. Enough is enough!

> **"...now the body is not for sexual immortality but for the Lord and the Lord for the body."** *I Corinthians 6:13*

As long as unwed, teenage girls continue to have babies, the vision of the next generation seems badly blurred. They are still girls themselves, in need mothers to raise them into womanhood. So how can we expect them to be mature enough to raise a baby on their own? Some families have abortions, while others bring unwanted babies into the world. If the only lifestyle that these under-aged parents know is struggle and poverty, their greatest motivation is survival. When hustling is the most available resource, what do you think that unwanted baby will grow up to learn? When I mention hustling, I'm not only speaking of organized crime and dealing drugs. Some mothers teach their own children how to hustle the system, not to mention how to use men to finance their materialistic needs. Statistics have proven that many teenage girls whose mothers had them at a young age are likely to repeat that same cycle. A vicious cycle, it is. Therefore, this repeated cycle often includes abuse and hopelessness. The hopelessness is brought on by the struggle—struggle to make ends meet, struggle to find a childcare in order to finish school or work, struggle to be a mother when she is still a child herself. If the father is not active in the child's life, without the support of someone, it becomes difficult for teenage mothers to reach their fullest educational and career potentials. We've got to make a change for this next generation of mothers. This cycle must come to an end.

I wish someone would have talked to me. I didn't know anything about protecting my virginity or my reputation, so I messed up way too early. No, I didn't get pregnant, by the grace of God, but I still have regrets. That's why it is of the utmost importance that mothers help our daughters be aware of the many woes of fornication. Motherhood is supposed to be a joy, and it is, when it happens at the proper time—when that girl becomes a woman, and is married and mentally ready for motherhood. This is not my order, but this is God's order.

So my question to mothers, hypothetically speaking, what signs do you think the mother of a pregnant teenager overlook? When, where, and how did that young girl's mother fall short? How could her involvement in her daughter's life have prevented this situation? Was her mother too un-involved in her daughter's day-to-day routine to see what was happening? Was her mother too strict that it pushed her daughter to rebel? Some questions are too difficult to answer. Besides, no one really knows the answer due to varying circumstances. So when I point the finger at mothers, it is not to say, "It's all our fault." It is merely to examine our roles in our children's lives, in order to ensure we support their development into young ladies, that they will make the best choices for themselves. If we don't stop messing around, making poor excuses in rearing our children, what will happen is: the teachings and influences from a "good mother" will diminish so severely that the mere concept of a "good mother" will be no more. All the world will have to offer is half-stepping mothers.

We already see that wise and seasoned grandmothers are becoming an endangered species.

Grandmothers today are so young that they don't have time to cook and prepare those delicious Sunday dinners, or to garden, or do any of the things, "old school" grandmothers use to do. This contributes to the fact that our youth today have little respect for the elderly and for authority, because back in the day "Big Mama" made sure she taught the grandchildren respect. These days, the only "Big Mama" or "Madea" we know of are Martin Lawrence and Tyler Perry. Mothers, let's slow down, reflect, and take a good look at ourselves.

To sum it up, whether mothers today lack spiritual direction, don't make time to properly raise their children, or don't know any better, it is my prayer that God's truth will saturate all of our hearts and ignite the positive, revolutionary transformation that needs to occur. We hope that those who can teach and offer insight to other mothers will have the required courage and influence to do so. We also hope and pray that mothers who half-step will recognize the need for change, and pray for God's strength in arriving to victory as a mother...in Jesus' name.

# Chapter 1 – Nurturing

As we begin exploring the many areas in which mothers must refrain from half-stepping, I have a parable to help us illustrate this process. (Jesus used parables to help us get it, right?) Well, let us imagine nursing a poor little flower back to health. In conjunction with the subject of this book, this flower will be symbolic of our need to restore the sicknesses and infirmities that exists in motherhood. This plant has been malnourished. It has suffered such turmoil and has become feeble, weak, and extremely delicate. In each of the upcoming six chapters, we will offer our flower the necessities for the restoration that it deserves, as we will also see clearly what is required of us as mothers.

Now, a plant needs to be nurtured. Aside from feeding it and giving it sunlight, some would argue that a flower will grow stronger, healthier and more beautiful if its care-giver would simply talk to it. So our first step in restoring our plant back to health is to _**nurture**_ _**our plant by providing water, sunlight, and kind words.**_ Talking to our fragile plant is part of the tender, nurturing process that many successful gardeners would not dare to neglect. Having a "green thumb" as they say, isn't enough. Many gardeners believe the results that come from talking to the plants would be detrimental to the outcome of the plant's growth and beauty.

Just like a flower, a child needs to be nurtured - mind, body, and spirit. So how does a mother like me begin? Well, let's begin at the beginning... breastfeeding. Uh-oh, there are a lot of women who came up during the women's rights era and they saw no importance of being held down like that. Then, there is the next generation of mothers who came up after the "bra-burners" who consequently never learned the importance of breastfeeding from their own mothers. Now, we have at least two generations of mothers who are unfamiliar with it, never saw anyone do it, and have no interest in giving it a second thought. The enemy has robbed us from one of the first crucial steps of nurturing from the very beginning and we must recognize this individually.

Aside from a physical incapability, why do so many women choose not to breast- feed? There are many mothers whose body unfortunately cannot produce enough milk for their child and would love to be able to breastfeed. On the other hand, there are some mothers who are selfish and just don't want to. Did I miss something or did God create our female bodies to grow into adulthood, developing breasts for a specific reason? So what's the reason; to look sexy for our man, or to feed our newly born children with the nutrients and immunities that they need? What's your answer to this question? Be honest now. If a mother is physically capable, at least for the first few weeks, if nothing else, why can't more mothers breast-feed? This will be bonding time to nurture your child, as well as giving them a jumpstart to a healthier life.

Now, it says something when the formula companies even admit that breastfeeding is better. Just read the labels, the first thing it reads is "For best results, breast milk is recommended." So what does that tell you? At least breastfeeding makes you have to hold your child in your arms. Many mothers who use bottles will simply lay the baby down and prop the bottle in the baby's mouth with a pillow. Now, this has completely eliminated the entire nurturing process for you and your baby, how sad. Mothers, I can talk about this because I'm guilty of this myself.

### *"Can a woman forget her nursing child?" Isaiah 49:15*

It is the trick of the enemy to lead us to believe that it is a mother's choice whether or not to breast feed, when her body can successfully produce good milk for the baby. Some mothers would give anything to nurse their children, but their bodies just won't allow it. So to those new mothers who are uncertain about their decision to breastfeed or use formula, I say to you, "don't half-step, do the right thing." It's not easy but it's worth it. Personally, I did not breast feed the whole first year, but at least, I breastfed as long as I could. I breastfed all four of my children and they did not have a lot of sicknesses during their first year of life. So again I say, it's not easy, but it is what God designed our bodies to do.

Ok, off the breast-feeding soap box. Next, on the subject of nurturing your children's physical bodies, let's look at the foods we feed them. Now mothers, I know most of us work and time does not always allow for home cooked meals everyday, but fast food everyday should not be the norm either. Hold on, before I go any further, I do not wish to hear any comments from the mother who so proudly proclaims, "I don't cook". As if it was something to brag on or be proud of. It is not cute to allow selfishness and laziness to lead us to raise our children on fast food everyday. Why can't fast food be a luxury, a treat, a reward for doing a good job, and occasionally the last resort on busy days? Mothers, if you feel you are simply not a good cook, so what? Your children will grow up thinking rice is supposed to be lumpy and they will love your ole nasty, lumpy rice. Besides, practice makes perfect.

Anything you stick with, you'll eventually get better at, right? Well, this is how we should look at cooking. All the grease and cholesterol from fast food will definitely hurt our children in the long run. Not to mention the steroids they put in the meat to make it so big. (...and we wonder why our children's bodies are developing so early.) We must love them enough to consider their eating habits; it's our jobs as their mothers. We can cook at night and heat it up the next day. Come on mothers, be creative.

When you think of the word nurturing, what comes to your mind? I think this is the one thing that separates what a mother can give verses what a father can give. Not to say a father is incapable; however, a real mother knows exactly where I'm going with this. It's deeper than a quick hug or a pat on the back. It withstands the test of time when all energy and patience is gone. It's just there. It is reliable and real, felt deeply within your soul. Why is this, "motherly duty", called nurturing so important? I say—because it is the evidence of love and every child deserves it.

So what exists today? What are half-stepping mothers today creating? They are creating children who don't know how to love. These children grow up to be adults who are so unfamiliar with the way love feels, that they find difficulty embracing love when it is presented to them. These are people who repeatedly choose to be involved with the wrong type of people, over and over. We all have someone we know who is "stuck on stupid" as they say, and continues to subject themselves to the same old thing in their romantic relationships. Why, one might ask? It's because they really don't know any better. They think abusive relationships are the reality for everyone. I have had someone really tell me, *"Girl, you don't love your man until you cut your man."* She meant, "cut" as in blood, knives and stitches. How dangerously scary is that? No matter how we point the finger and criticize this mindset, it exists.

Another result of nurturing neglect is one that I feel is very important. Mothers today do not encourage their children enough. Believe me, the world will give them all the insults, criticism, and negativity they would ever imagine, but at least, your children should know that Mama believes in them. Half the mothers today beat their children down with harsh words more than anyone else. What's wrong with that picture? You see, when you plant positivity in the hearts of your children, then this is what they will subconsciously believe. So who cares when the bully at the lunch table is checking her and calling her skinny? In the back of her mind, she remembers her mother's words about how she is fearfully and wonderfully made. She will remember how God made her small to prove how special she really was, not like all the rest. This is how she is able to totally ignore criticism and remain confident about herself. Why, because her Mama believes in her and tells her she is the best.

This is why we must certainly ensure that we nurture our children's spiritual growth. It would be difficult to tell our children what God thinks about them if we don't know what God thinks about us. We must nurture the development of our children's prayer lives and their knowledge of scripture. It is our duty to nurture their spiritual character as they grow, but it first starts with us. We must show them more than we tell them. Often time, our children learn by watching us. Our words are very important because faith comes by hearing; however, our actions speak much louder than words.

After looking at the need for nurturing our children and at some of the benefits and negative outcomes, let's peek into the archives of how Sister Young nurtured her children.

# Sister Young's Way

Sister Young did, indeed, possess a natural, nurturing quality. She nurtured your spirit, she cultivated your will to try and you felt God's love through her. How did she do this? She never missed the opportunity to do so. If you needed an encouraging word, she said it. If you needed a hug, she gave it. If you were hungry, she feed you. If you needed clothing or shelter, you could find it in her. She nurtured everyone, not just her own children. She made time for you. Some people never received this type of love before and for some, never again. Nonetheless, they would never be the same because they got a taste from sweet Sister Young.

Let's look at how she nurtured one of her own. Her oldest daughter, Joy, spoke so fondly of her mother. When I interviewed Joy, her first response was *"My mother was my friend."* Not in a way that many mothers have become tricked in today's society. Some mothers today try too hard to assume the role of friend and let the role of mother slip right between their fingers. Sister Young knew that she was mother first, but she shared a level of compassion which made her children feel her friendship and respect.

The problem we see today with mothers who think they are their children's friends is the fact that these mothers let their children argue with and disrespect them. Children want a real mother in their lives. They will meet many friends but they have only one mother. It's time for us mothers to re-define what motherhood really means.

Yes, Sister Young definitely used an old fashion conversation as a channel to nurture her children. This was the time her daughter Joy remembered Sister Young teaching her many day-to-day values. This is the stuff, as they say, "...your Mama should have taught you." For example, back then many women wore hair rollers. Unfortunately, many women never heard their mother tell them not to wear hair rollers in public. (Since hair rollers are not very popular today, let's equate this to people in public with pajamas and house shoes.) Sister Young taught Joy how to conduct herself as a lady. This level of self-respect that Joy learned from her mother strongly affected her. She not only learned things from her mother's teaching but also from her mother's own behaviors. Because Sister Young was such a good example to Joy, it led Joy to always strive to be a good example to her two younger sisters.

Joy remembered the challenge of speaking in front of an audience when she was growing up. She remembered an incident at church where she was supposed to read the announcements and she absolutely froze. She was so nervous that the words would not come out. Joy was devastated but her mother reminded her, *"at least you tried".* She encouraged her to keep trying and soon she wouldn't even be affected by her nerves and fears. Conversations like this was why Joy considered her mother to be her friend.

Joy remembered the fear of telling her mother of her plans for college. Not only was Joy beautiful and talented, but she was also very intelligent. Joy was one of those graduating seniors that most colleges and universities wanted to recruit. With all of these choices, the thought choosing a local university seemed to be mediocre. When Joy gained the courage to share her decision to stay home and attend the University of Memphis, Sister Young quickly rejoiced with her. This meant the world to Joy and was a refreshing relief. Sister Young nurtured Joy's confidence to make her own decision. She respected her decision to choose her own college and this proved that Sister Young was Joy's friend since she considered Joy's wishes above anyone else's opinion.

Sister Young put her children first. The nurturing she gave helped to build their confidence because they were not rejected by their mother. If she was engaged in conversation with someone and one of the children came to her with an emergency, she would excuse herself and briefly give her child her attention. Obviously, the emergencies were often trivial; nonetheless, this created a sense of worth within each of her children. How many times have we heard a mother say to her child, *"Be quiet, don't you see grown folks talking?"* Yes, we should teach our children to show respect, but shouldn't we also respect them as human beings? Something to think about, huh?

Encouragement, encouragement, encouragement is what Sister Young gave her children. She kept them involved and she pushed them to try. When opportunities were presented, she made sure her children took advantage of them. No room for shyness, no room for low self-esteem, and no room for laziness. If there was down time, she had them reading or doing something constructive. This built character within them.

There's no surprise that she nurtured their spiritual life. She covered them in prayer daily. She also took it upon herself to develop their prayer life and knowledge of the Word of God. She was consistent with her family Bible Studies and enforcement of memory verses that helped to build spiritual understanding and their personal relationship with God. These were simple ways that Sister Young consistently nurtured her children.

---

Discussion:
- Identify and discuss ways to nurture children of various ages.
- What is your personal scripture of promise that addresses the need to nurture your child(ren)?

# Chapter 2 – Guidance

To GUIDE SOMETHING OR someone means to lead it in a certain direction. Now that we have nurtured the plant back to health, it still needs strong guidance. Instead of growing straight up, our flower is leaning off to the wayside. ***The next step in growing our plant is to place a stick firmly into the dirt to act as <u>guidance</u> for the flower to grow upright and strong.*** The stick's mission is to guide the flower in the right direction. The stick will be such an influence on the flower that soon the flower will no longer need the stick. Soon the flower will stand alone and exemplify the guidance that was gathered from the stick. This example is a simple technique for nurturing a flower but for a child, providing guidance is a never-ending process.

How many times have we heard someone say, *"He was a good child, but I don't know what happened?"* The question is, at what point did you stop guiding your child? As the over-seer of our children, it is our role to guide them in their decisions and choices in life. How many times did you recognize that your child was beginning to stray away from your positive or Godly path? Did you, as the mother, take control by providing parental guidance? It is then that we should intervene by giving mandatory instructions that will get our children back on track. We shouldn't feel guilty about doing this. Remember, we are the parents and we reserve the right.

Some parents feel that once their children reach a certain age, they can make their own decisions about everything—from what they eat, to how they dress, to where they go. Some parents even ask their child, "Are you going to church today?" As parents, some of us have truly "punked out". We are afraid to set limits and standards. However, the truth of the matter is, even if the answer is "no", your child will still love you. Sure they might be disappointed, but the sooner you teach your child how to accept the word "no" the easier it will be later on in life.

It's also good to respect your child enough to explain why the best answer for them is "no." I personally don't agree with the statement, *"Because I'm the parent and I said so, that's why."* If you show guidance by explaining to your child why you told them "no", then they can comprehend why "no" was the best choice. Soon they will be able to make their own decisions pertaining to similar matters with the same wisdom.

An example that quickly comes to mind deals

with the TV shows that I allow my children to watch. We all know that all cartoons are not good cartoons. Well, there are a few cartoons that I noticed encourage witchery, sorcery, and other unfavorable things. There were two cartoons that were very popular when my children were younger that gave me a bad vibe. So, I began to say to my children, *"Uuuuhhh, that's the stinky, nasty cartoon. We don't like that cartoon."* So, I would either turn the TV off or change the channel to another cartoon. One day, it was TV time and the children were watching TV as I cooked. Suddenly, my oldest son ran into the kitchen to warn me, *"Mom, hurry, hurry look what's on TV. Come change the channel."* This was a small way that my parental guidance for my children to avoid being negatively influenced by certain TV shows had taught my son how to make his own decisions. He had no desire to sneak and watch it because his interest had been guided in another direction.

Children can feel your love when they know your guidance on certain situations stem from you desiring what is best for them. Besides, how can we say we love our children if we don't care what he or she does, how he or she acts, where he or she goes and so on? When I was a child, I use to think kids were lucky when their parents allowed them the freedom to hang out after school. However, these were the children that grew up too fast and took the wrong paths in life. The reality is, if there are rules in place for your child to come home by a certain time, do household chores, do all their homework and studying, study the scriptures and pray, eat dinner, prepare for the next day, and go to sleep on time, then there is little time for all the trouble that's in the streets, on the internet, or on TV. You are simply guiding your child down a different path than mothers who have no rules for their children to follow each day. It's not hard to establish these kinds of rules because these are things they should be doing anyway, so how can they argue? It makes them learn how to be responsible and it also teaches time management at an early age. Children don't need too much idle or free time. The lack of structure or rules is what the enemy uses to get a child in trouble. The way to fight against the devil's plan to get our children in trouble is by providing the proper guidance to steer them down the proper path. Guidance is crucial in raising a child, so mothers, please don't half-step with the guidance.

God knew the children of Israel needed guidance so He gave them the Ten Commandments. As a parent, we should have certain rules in our home that cannot be broken, as well. God also took it a step farther when He gave us the Holy Spirit to dwell in us. So when you hear someone say, "*I had a funny feeling about that*" or

*"Something told me not to do that"*; it is the Holy Spirit acting as our guide. Sure, we can teach our children good virtues and morals in life but the best thing is to guide our children to be in tune with the Holy Spirit's direction.

So mothers, know that we are half-stepping if we don't provide guidance when we see something that is negatively influencing our children. These are mothers who do not lift a finger to guide their children back on track once they see them beginning bad habits. Some of these bad habits include; hanging with bad company, using bad language, dressing and looking weird, or bringing home bad report cards. Woops, hold up, stop the presses—let's talk about bad report cards.

I would like to put all mothers "on blast", or in the "hot-seat", if you will, who half-step in the area of education. These are the mothers who show no involvement the entire grading period but when the report cards come out, they march up to the school and curse the teachers out for not telling them their child was struggling. Why is there so little guidance when it comes to our parental roles in tutoring, studying, reading, comprehending, and learning? This is our children's education, for goodness sake. We should be assisting with projects, studying with them, helping them prepare for tests, exams and even quizzes.

Mothers, we need to commit to mandatory homework time at least three nights a week. Seriously? Even if you don't completely understand or can't really grasp the lessons, then learn with your children. If your child did not take good enough notes to be able to come home and teach you what the teacher taught them, then they are not paying attention in class themselves and shame on them. What better indicator of their behavior in class? These lessons may be new to you, but if your household rule is to bring home all books and classroom lecture notes, then you both can read the lessons and learn together. I, for one, thought it was cruel that my parents made me bring home all my books everyday so they could go over every subject with me. I was the only student in the class who had to bring home every single book. Even when the teacher said, "No homework, class," I still had to bring home every book. I thought I had the meanest parents in the world. Little did I know, that my parents were simply teaching me strong study habits. You shouldn't wait until the night before a test to study. Although I didn't like it at all, I formally thank you, Mr. and Mrs. DeBerry, for your parental guidance in the area of my education.

There are too many mothers who have no idea what their children are studying in math right now, or what they are reading about in history, or what science project is due next week. The children have no support or accountability at home, so why bother?

Three nights a week, mothers. It should be non-negotiable. Now does that sound like too much to ask? As a matter of fact, you can have a scripture lesson before and a prayer after you study. Your children will love you for this quality time together and they will be inspired to make you proud by bringing home better grades. We can't put all the responsibility on the teachers. How can teachers give your child the personal attention they need when the teachers have twenty-five plus students in each class. So ladies, don't half-step, guide your children's education both scholastically and spiritually. Guide them in their interests, their habits, and especially their goals in life. There's no room for half-stepping in the area of guidance. We must start early preparing them for the rest of their lives.

# Sister Young's Way

There are so many ways a person can take when traveling. There are also many things that can entice a person to choose a certain path. The route could be shorter, less traffic, newer roads, more lanes, faster speed limits, and so on. Nonetheless, the right path for you is the right path for you. Satan will make all the other paths appear to be so nice and comfortable but face it, if it's not the right path for you, it must be the wrong path. The enemy will always tempt our children to get off track because that's his job and we should expect that. The question is, will we let our children "go out like that" (off path) or will we fight for them by providing "guidance" to steer them back on track?

One thing, I must say about Sister Young, she figured out the best road map for her family was the Bible. She always taught them to live their lives according to the Bible's instructions. She taught them that God's way was the best way. She gave them hope that a fulfilling life can be for all God's people who reverence Him first. So, the first act of guidance was to guide her children to the Lord. She always witnessed the gospel to them and to their friends. With love, she always spread the good news of hope, love and salvation through Christ our Savior.

There are some things that just naturally happen. Some people may be a little clumsy or some people are loud and obnoxious. This doesn't make them bad people, but these traits, if not controlled early on, could develop into bad habits. Camille, the baby girl, remembers being a child who loved to sleep. There are people who really do sleep their lives away, so yes, this could have been a bad trait to develop. It could also turn into laziness later in life. Well, Sister Young recognized this quality in her little "Peanut", as they called Camille. She recognized that she needed to help guide Camille to change this natural occurrence. There are a lot of half-stepping mothers out there who would let their children sleep all the time just to keep the children from bothering them. The bottom line, however, is that laziness is a sin.

> *"How long will you slumber, O sluggard? When will you rise from your sleep?" Proverb 6:9*

Camille also remembers her mother's ability to guide each of them into their destiny. Camille was blessed with a beautiful singing voice. Her voice began to develop and mature at a young age. Sister Young cultivated this gift by encouraging Camille to lead songs in the church choir, even as young as four years old. Today, Camille is a renown soloist in the Memphis Area. She is one of the featured vocalists in the *Annual Young Family Concert* that draws a packed house each year. All of this is much to her mother's credit by guiding Camille into her gift.

Sister Young also showed guidance by not allowing the children to argue. With six children in the house, we would all imagine that there would be a lot of arguing, but that was not the case at all. Sister Young did not play that. If there was an argument, she would bring them together and get to the bottom of what happened. She taught the children how to respect each other and, in turn, she was subliminally teaching them how to love each other. Whoever was responsible for starting the argument got in trouble. This shows that Sister Young did not take yelling and bickering lightly. Think about it—if a child got in trouble for mistreating their siblings the same way they would get in trouble for such things as missing curfew, maybe they might learn to respect their siblings a little more. If mothers held that much weight on arguing, instead of just letting their children have battling matches, maybe we can guide them to have a friendlier sibling relationship. Sister Young taught her children to be good neighbors to their siblings. This made it easier for them to grow up to have good relationships as adults. The devil's ploy is to stir up confusion and chaise in our homes through sibling rivalry. The peace of God that was within Sister Young helped her to know that sibling rivalry did not have to exist in her home. She guided her children in the direction of peace.

Sister Young had no problem stepping in and offering guidance to her beloved children. As a mother, she felt it her duty to do so. She also guided them along academically. Her involvement in the PTA made her knowledgeable of activities and programs for her children. She guided their desire to participate in constructive arenas that made good use of their time. She also guided them to be actively involved in ministry. She made it fun. Sister Young's approach was to guide the children down the path of sisterly and brotherly love. It is a joy to watch and a sight to see how her children continue to travel that same path of peace, even today.

In the journey of life, Sister Young was the tour guide for her children. A bad tour guide can make the journey boring and lifeless; but a good guide makes it worth the trip. Considering the way Sister Young offered guidance while raising her children; let's just say Sister Young made the journey unforgettable.

---

Discussion:
- Identify and discuss ways to offer guidance for children of various ages.
- What is your personal scripture of promise that addresses the need to give guidance to your child(ren)?

# Chapter 3 – Training

NOW HERE'S A SUBJECT that we hear a lot, don't you think? Have you ever heard someone say, *"Now that child just has no home-training?"* Well, I sure have and I've also said it. If the child really had no home-training, whose fault is that? That's what I thought, the parents fault. Ok mothers, we have a lot to address on this subject.

It's good to call it "home-training" because it should begin at home. Training is something we never stop doing, no matter how old the child gets. We should always remember, this child never asked to be here. Therefore, it is our full and total responsibility to train and teach this sweet little person everything they need to know. There are some things that will require us to stay on them. By that I mean repeat training, practice with them, remind them, correct them, applaud them, reiterate, explain, reinforce—you get the picture. Children today have so many things fighting against their ability to grasp things the first time you tell them. The enemy can use things like rebellion, impatience, creativity, or your child might just be, as the older folks say, "plain hard-headed."

I haven't even mentioned the ADHD epidemic. Whatever the case may be, if you stay on them hard enough and consistently enough, they will adapt to your way. Just like training a pet, a good parent can condition their children to act, speak, behave, and sometimes think a certain way. Mothers, how much time and effort have you really put into training your children?

> **"Train up a child in the way he should go, and when he is old he will not depart from it. Proverb 22:6.**

What do you think the word "train" really means in that scripture? How important is this five letter word? Well, let's go back to the plant that we are growing. In the last chapter, we used a stick for guidance because the plant was leaning to the wayside. Now, we must train the plant to follow the lead of the stick. *Therefore, in this step, we must tightly and securely tie the plant close to the stick, in our effort to <u>train</u> the plant to grow upward and accept the guidance of the stick.*

There is great significance in the words "tightly" and "securely". If we tied the plant to the stick softly and loosely, we would not get the same effect of tying the plant tightly. Tying it tightly increases our chances that the plant will be trained to grow upward. If we tied the plant loosely, it would increase the chances of the plant growing back off track again. So in raising our children, we must take the "tightly tied" approach, don't you think? We certainly don't want them to grow off track again. They can easily go back to the wayside, if we turn our back. So, it's up to us to tie our rope of parental training as tightly as possible, to teach our children that abiding by our training is the only thing that we will accept. We must certainly pay attention to their progress. The only way we can "inspect what we expect" is to spend time with the children, pay attention to them, talk to them, and find out what's really going on.

The half-stepping mother ties her rope loosely. She yells and screams at the children, giving some training and some teaching, but the consistency and follow-up is not there. It's hard for the children to really take Mama seriously when the child knows that she won't follow up. Children become immune to all the yelling when they know it won't go any farther than that. Even with training a dog, it takes repeat follow up, repeat practice, repeat discipline and repeat rewards for the dog to truly catch on to a certain behavior.

**"You shall teach them diligently to you children, and shall talk of them when you sit in your house, when you walk by the way, when you lie down, and when you rise up." Deuteronomy 6:7**

So mothers, if we want our children to learn how to sit down and only whisper in church or in a restaurant, we should practice that at home. Perhaps you and your child can sit down on the couch and do a few practice runs on sitting quietly. Only allow your child to whisper if he or she must say something. Give him or her something to write or draw, but begin to really train your child the practice of sitting quietly. When Sunday rolls around, refer to what you expect before you walk into the church and your child just might surprise you. Children love the pride of accomplishment. Make sure you reward them for their good, quiet behavior. Don't forget, rewarding your child could merely be a high-five or their favorite drink from the corner store. It does not have to be costly, but simply recognize what they have done right and they will continue to want to make you proud.

When we see children who exhibit poor behavior, in many cases, it is a reflection of the parents. Face it, a child comes into the world wretched, undone, and seeking direction. It is the parents' responsibility to teach that child everything he needs to learn. When the parent sends the child out into the world, he becomes an example of what he has been taught, but, in order to learn a thing, one must have a teacher. So who holds the primary responsibility of being your child's teacher? Heather, I'm glad you asked that question.

Mothers, we have a big job on our hands. Now, I'm not suggesting that we can train our children to never stray or be disobedient. (We, as adults are disobedient, as well.) However, that which we deeply instill in our children, we pray that the Holy Spirit will convict them to do. It is our role to be consistent in our teaching. When my second son was about three years old, I don't know how many times I've had to remind him to cover his mouth and say excuse me when he sneezed. Sometimes he would remember and I would say, "good job saying excuse me" but when he forgot, I would always verbally discipline him not to forget how it's done. So when he would be out in public and he covered his mouth and said "excuse me", a bystander would think, *"That little boy has great manners."* The bystander would not be interested in how many times it took me to remind him to always cover his mouth; all that mattered was that my three year old has been taught.

So, we know this training process is forever. It must be a daily, every day, all day, day in and day out practice. It takes commitment and consistency. It's not easy for a mother or father, but if you truly love your child, training them and preparing them for life is what we must all stick to.

For best results, the secret to this is consistent training. Mothers, we must set the expectation and be on their behinds when they get caught slipping. *"If there is no accountability, expect no results."* Hold up Mothers, stop and think about what that really means. What this is really saying to Mothers is simple, but profound. To establish the needed accountability when training our children, mothers must begin paying more attention to their children, period, point blank. We tune our children out. They could be calling our name ten times before we even hear them. On the contrary, training out children has to be a full time, all the time job.

A drill sergeant can only successfully train his troops if he watches for accuracy. Am I correcting in saying that? I never served in the military, but I survived eighteen years with my father, a twenty-two year Army Vet and he was the king of drill sergeants, in my opinion. There was only two ways of doing things, Mr. D's way or the wrong way. He didn't let up on his standards and I appreciate him for it today. (Thanks Daddy!) We must learn to be better drill sergeants. We cannot continue putting in a little here and a little there in training our children; yet, we must focus our attention on ensuring they learn life lessons as they grow and mature.

So, how can a coach develop his team players?

How will the players really know that they are doing it right? The answer is training and feedback. How can parents train their child, or offer the quote/unquote "home-training," that they need if the parents never follow-up on what is expected. Merely looking in on the children, every now and then, will not work any longer. Our children's future is at stake. We must give them as close to undivided attention as we possibly can. Yes, I know we, as mothers, have a lot on our plates so, we must brush up on our own "multi-tasking skills". It's up to us to let our children know when they are acting or behaving less than what is expected. If we half-step in the area of training, we will risk the chance of negative behaviors becoming the person that our children grow up to be.

# Sister Young's Way

How many of us have two or more children and we are pulling our hair out trying to handle them? Well, my husband and I have four children, who are now ages 12, 10, 7, and 2, so I agree; it is not a walk in the park. If we parents have allowed our children to become "spoiled" and "disorderly", then training them can be a real challenge. So, how was Sister Young able to handle six children so well? I know one thing, the fact that her children had home-<u>training</u> made it less chaotic. Let's look at how she trained her six, stair-step children.

Well, Sister Young's six children were not unruly or defiant, yet Kevin admits that he did not always make things simple for Sister Young. Nonetheless, Sister Young had an unequal but fair way of training her children that worked well. You see, no two children are ever alike and it takes more for some and less for others. Kevin remembers his mother taking up more time with him often. He had certain distractions that made it more difficult to bring home the good report cards like some of his siblings. The first thing that he remembers is his love for candy. All of that sugar makes a child hyper. Who can calmly sit down and learn when the sugar makes them want to run wild. Well, that was the circumstance in most cases with Kevin. He remembers his mother staying on him about eating candy all the time, but Kevin was as they say, "hard-headed."

With Kevin, there were often times when Sister Young would simply ask him, *"Kevin, what were you thinking?"* Yes, she had to stay on him, but this did not mean constant yelling and criticizing. No, she was consistent with him, but she was also patient. It is our impatience that leads to all of the fussing and hollering. This is not always the best approach. Instead of leading the child to understand what you are trying to convey, it can sometime lead your child to shut down, lash back or rebel. Think about it, if someone is yelling at you, your first, natural reaction is to jump on the defense. Sister Young avoided that by reprimanding with love.

> *"...do not provoke your child to wrath,*
> *but bring them up in the training and*
> *admonition of the Lord." Ephesians 6:4*

In this scripture, (Eph 6:4), the word admonition means mild, kind, yet earnest reproof. Now this just sounds like Sister Young: no screaming, no cursing, no throwing stuff; just mild, kind reproof.

Kevin also remembers the fact that his mother took time to help him build confidence in learning, in spite of his stuttering disability. He remembers in 7th grade, he brought home two F's on his report card. Sister Young did not hit the roof; she was understanding. Instead of blowing up and going off, she increased her one-on-one time tutoring him at home. She pushed him to work harder and in the 8th grade Kevin made the Honor Roll. Sister Young absolutely rejoiced. Her excitement for him encouraged him to continue to strive for excellence in school.

Kevin recalls several ways that his mother trained her children. She taught them how to be organized and have good time-management skills. She would place a schedule on the refrigerator for daily duties around the house and other activities. Working from a written schedule or to-do list is a simple practice that many children are never exposed to. Me personally, I was an adult well into my career before I attended a time management class to learn what the Youngs were taught at a young age.

Above all, Kevin remembers his mother conducting formal bible studies and requiring them to learn memory verses. They would go around the table and recite a verse every night before dinner. She not only trained their minds, she trained their hearts. She spent time teaching them about manners and values in life. She talked to them. She even taught the boys how to treat a lady and made them practice on her and their sisters. Things like opening doors and being a gentleman became things that the boys simple did because their Mama trained them that way. They learned to be gentlemen just like learning to walk and talk. It was mandatory in Sister Young's opinion. That's probably why the three boys turned out to be such charming, sophisticated men, even until this day.

Sister Young never stopped with the training. She was consistent and she met her children where they were. Uncle Sonnie, Sister Young's brother fondly spoke of her self- proclaimed "six personalities". Sister Young knew she had to be a different mother for each of her six children, in order to meet each of their needs fully. Sister Young kept a mental record of the different areas that her children needed more focus toward. She knew her children's strengths and weaknesses and she offered training to each of them accordingly. It's incredible to believe that in all of my interviews with the siblings, each and every one of her children felt that she always made time for them. That is absolutely remarkable.

In the same manner, we must pay close attention to our children's areas of development. Whether it is hygiene or diet or manners or certain subjects in school, we must evaluate what's really going on. This will make it clear to us, as parents, exactly how to train them in areas that will benefit them. Teaching all the children the same thing in the same way may not always be most effective. Therefore, it is important to find ways to meet the needs of each child individually.

So yes, Sister Young did have her hands full. Even though Sister Young was involved in many activities and in the lives of so many people; nothing came before her role as mother of her six children. Raising her children was her priority and she loved it more than anything else. To the average person, what Sister Young accomplished just seems like too much to even strive for. Her commitment to God made it all possible for her and if we, likewise, commit ourselves to God wholeheartedly, He will order our steps in the way of victory as it relates to our children.

---

Discussion:
- Identify and discuss ways to offer train children of various ages.
- What is your personal scripture of promise that addresses the need to train your child(ren)?

# Chapter 4 – Discipline

THERE ARE TWO MEANINGS for the word discipline that quickly comes to mind. One meaning is, "orderly training" and the other meaning is, "punishment." Now, with our plant, after the proper <u>nurturing</u>, <u>guidance</u> and <u>training,</u> to regain its strength to grow upright and strong, we now notice that our plant has begun growing grass and weeds all around it. Now, this is to be expected. As with raising children, there will always be distractions that the enemy will use to get us off track. The weeds exemplify wildness and freedom that rises up naturally. However, the weeds will take from the neat, orderly look that we are working toward. ***Therefore, we must physically pull the weeds up to maintain the health and beauty of our plant.***

As we compare raising a child to this plant of ours, there will be many "weeds" that will grow all around our children. Again, this is to be expected. The enemy is not going to just sit and let you be a positive influence in your child's life and not try to shake things up a bit. His job is to play defense to every offensive play that you call. That's why a good, strong block player must be on our team. Of course, the parent has to be the coach and the block but its ok, that's just how it is.

### *"...Things that cause people to stumble are bound to come..." Luke 17:1*

Imagine a family household that usually keeps the TV on all day. If a child is used to watching cartoons all day, their mind becomes somewhat hyper. Sometime, the fast pace of the cartoons on TV makes the children want to run and jump and be very active; therefore, doing something as calm as reading or studying can appear to be too boring for this child. It's amazing how calm your house would be if you did one simple thing, turn off the TV! We train our children how to waste time by keeping this enticing distraction going from the time we wake up until we fall asleep. Some people even sleep with it on all night. For a young child, the sooner they are taught how to control their conduct, the better. It is the parent's job to pull the weeds in situations just like this. We should control things like TV, video games, computer, iPads, and cell phones. They may not like it, but they must learn balance as early as possible.

One way of developing this particular discipline is by having designated time to read, study, or even play quietly. For so long, I thought my two oldest kids were wild just because they were boys. Then came my first daughter who now holds the title, "Wildest of Them All". Even when I would read books to them, they were too hyper. The reality was, we had to teach them how to be quiet sometimes. So at the end of the night before bed, they had two options, either play quietly in their room or go to bed early. I'm sure you can imagine which one they choose. The first time they got loud, off to bed they went. They understood the consequence of their actions and they soon learned how to play quietly. Now they are familiar with "quiet play" and when it is time for quiet time, they accept it. Had I never exposed them to quiet play then they would have never developed this discipline.

A disciplined mind can handle loud, energetic activities as well as quiet, calm activities. It is up to us as parents to teach our children this type of balance. They are not going to learn it on their own. Don't expect them to sit in a nice restaurant and behave in a mature manner if you have never practiced this behavior with them. My two middle children are so loud that I have to practice their whispering techniques at home. They still haven't mastered whispering, but we're working on it.

There's nothing wrong with kids being kids, running around and being loud when the time and location allows. There's a time and place for everything and they must learn and practice this.

> **"To everything there is a season, a time for every purpose under heaven." Eccles 3:1**

Now, let's look at the other meaning of the word discipline; punishment. So many parents fuss and correct too much and others not enough. Many people agree that the condition of today's youth is a result of poor discipline in their homes. If children do not listen to their own mother or father, what makes us believe they will respect any authority at all? This is a problem that must be addressed at home first. Mothers, don't half-step, if your children get out of line, it's your job to check 'em. By that I mean, corporal punishment in your own way. Yeah, I said it. With all the controversy about spanking your children, it's just one of those things that you don't enjoy, but it's just part of it. Whether your version of a spanking is one or two licks or if you really get them good, this is a way for your child to respect authority and to help them make decisions that won't result in a spanking. Spankings are not a tool for the parent to exert frustrations. To me, that's child abuse. Don't take your own anger out on your children for reasons such as mistakes or accidents. Children will be children. We, as parents, should question our own level of training and teaching before we condemn our children for making mistakes. Use compassion, but don't ever spare the rod. This sends mixed messages that you don't mean business and that's the last thing you want to indicate to your child.

I've heard so many parents say, *"If you do that one more time, I'm gonna get you,"* but the child does it five more times and never gets anything. This half-stepping parent is too soft-hearted to spank their child and ends up spoiling their child. No one purposely leaves a full gallon of milk out to spoil, so why do we spoil our children? When I say spoil, I don't mean loving your child dearly and buying them things to make them happy or look nice. There's nothing wrong with this if they have been good and obedient children and you feel they deserve these acts of reward. Webster describes the word "spoiled" as damaged, ruined, and decayed. Our children can become damaged, ruined, and decayed in their behavior. This will happen to our children if the parents lack the courage to use the rod of authority in their lives.

> *"Whoever spares the rod hates their children, but the one who loves their children is careful to discipline them. Proverbs 13:24*

If we love our children, we should show it by effectively disciplining them. This includes discipline over their leisure activities, how much they eat, how they behave, their daily routines and responsibilities and so on. If parents step in and regulate certain consistencies in the children's lives, we can easily measure the difference you see in their behavior. All that fussing and yelling means nothing after a while. There comes a time when you have to take action to really prove your point. Pray and ask God to show you how to discipline your children and have the courage and commitment to stick to it. Remember, just because they took prayer and spankings out of school does not mean you should stop doing it at home. Don't half-step, take control over your children's behavior before it's too late!

*"Chasten your son while there is hope, and do not set your heart on his destruction." Proverb 19:18*

# SISTER YOUNG'S WAY

YOU KNOW, THERE WAS a time when people could leave their children playing in the front yard, no matter what neighborhood. These were the days when neighbors were considered family and they all looked out for everyone's children. Neighbors protected their safety and they even provided discipline when needed. Today, you better not say anything to someone else's child, and don't even think about chastising them. You can barely punish your own children in public. You can't as much as thump them without DHS blowing the whistle on you claiming "unnecessary roughness".

There are many things in life that has changed from the good ole days, way back when. However, just as the Word of God stays the same, there are certain things in life that shouldn't change in your homes and disciplining your child is one of them. Let me tell you about Sister Young's approach on the subject. Let's just say, she didn't mind spanking that behind every now and again. Just ask her eldest son Steve, he can tell you all about it.

Now Steve was a handful. He quickly admitted

that fact. Sister Young, however, had something for him every time. For Steve, it finally sunk in and he grew up to be the Pastor of the same church his father planted. Sister Young could have thrown her hands in the air and given up, but she stuck with him, and if she were here today, she would be proud of the man he turned out to be.

So many mothers today give up too quickly. Children are going to do things that are simply unthinkable.

### *"Foolishness is bound in the heart of a child..." Proverb 22:15*

If you give a child an inch, we all know the child will take a mile. This is no mystery. Therefore mothers, we cannot give up on enforcing strict discipline. Oh no, we must be consistent with the consequences of their actions. If the Bible tells us that it's ok to spank your child, then who are we to question that?

### *"Do not withhold correction from a child. For, if you beat him with a rod, he will not die." Proverbs 23:13*

Steve's memory of his mother as it relates to discipline was pretty simple. *"Mama never held back the strap."* Even with a personality of such kindness and patience, Sister Young's discipline was just as consistent. Steve remembered, however, his mother explaining to him how she would much rather talk with him than to spank him. He was the first to admit that it took the strap for him, as his mother's attempts to talk and reason with him only went in one ear and out the other. Sister Young would often find out why before she jumped to conclusions. She did make every effort to offer leniency toward her children before she resorted to the strap. On the other hand, Steve's account of spankings from his mother out-numbered his father ten to one. Even though she was extremely kind to the children, the need for corporal punishment was still present and Sister Young did not half-step.

Steve remembered a particular lesson in discipline that stayed with him his entire life. Although it did not involve a rod, switch, or belt, it was still a very painful punishment that became a permanent life lesson for him.

Steve had noticed that one of his friends had created a collection of *Sports Illustrated* swimsuit centerfold models on his wall. The boy told him that he had been secretively stealing the photos from the library. So one day, Steve and some friends were walking down to the library, as they often did, and the thought entered Steve's mind to get a photo for his bedroom wall. When Sister Young noticed the picture and questioned Steve about it, she had the perfect way to teach Steve a lesson on stealing. She made Steve take the picture back to the library, confess and apologize to the librarian, and do community service there at the library. Steve was embarrassed, of course, but he learned his lesson and never forgot that stealing was strictly prohibited in the Young's household. This was also a lesson to his friends. Until this day, Steve and his friends have fond memories of that situation.

Steve remembered his mother staying on him about doing his best. She could recognize when he had not applied himself and she always pushed him to reach a little higher. She tried to instill in him the self-discipline to strive for that which God had embedded within Steve and the others.

One thing Steve said that touched me deeply was the fact that he remembered the fun that he had with his mother far more than he remembered negative interactions such as spankings. He remembered how she would chase him through the house and tickle them. He remembered the hugs she gave, the funny faces she would make, the kisses and her love. Steve explained, *"Mama's love was so good that we didn't want it to stop...that's why we really hated to see her upset with us."* This statement convinces me that no matter how much it hurts us to discipline our children, it will never influence or take from the love that our children will have toward us. It is when harsh discipline is the only interaction between a parent and a child that it becomes abusive. Abuse can make a child resent a parent. On the other hand, when a child feels love from a parent, that child will learn to understand that discipline is just another fruit that grows from the tree of love. In the end, the fruit of discipline is just as sweet.

*"Those whom I love I rebuke and discipline." Revelations 3:19*

---

Discussion:

- Identify and discuss ways to discipline children of various ages. Identify ways to teach them self-discipline.
- What is your personal scripture of promise that addresses the need to discipline your child(ren)?

# Chapter #5 – Affection

WOULD YOU LOOK AT this? Our flower is now standing tall. The withered pedals are now perky. The dull colors are now illuminant. There's no need for a stick to guide it—it can now stand alone. All the nurturing, guidance, training, and discipline have worked. Oh, how proud you must feel, knowing that your hard work was not in vain. You know what this calls for? This calls for a moment to show how proud you are. What better way to show your admiration than to do a little bragging—a little showing off? I mean, why not? You have invested a lot of time and energy, right? Now your hard work has reaped a beautiful reward. Why not show somebody? If the flower could feel, it would feel your affection toward it. **Therefore, in this step, we will express our <u>affection</u> towards the flower by taking it outside and showing it off.** Let's look at how this relates to raising children.

Affection, the subject of this chapter, is often overlooked by many mothers. Sometimes a mother has to do what a mother has to do, which may mean being a mother and a father. Single mothers know exactly where I'm going with this. Much like the nurturing chapter, affection can be misconstrued with the ulterior motive to raise your boys to be men, to be tough, to be strong. However, showing affection toward your children will not make them weak; it will merely make them emotionally strong. Affection is the manifestation of love. It is the tangible, embodiment of the phrase, "I love you." I am in no way undermining the importance of sternly guiding your children into adulthood. However, when we associate affection with "babying" our children, then there's a problem.

Speaking of "babying"; think back to how life is with a brand new baby in the house. No, I'm not talking about the bad stuff. Let's only focus on the warm and fuzzy. Allow me to paint the picture.

We now have this sweet little baby girl in our home. Oh, what a bundle of joy. She is so soft, smelling like baby lotion. She is generous with the eye contact and the smiles. We, mothers, want nothing more than to care for her all day. Imagine the hugs, the kisses, the way her tiny, little head feels laying on our necks. It is our pleasure, as a mother, to show affection toward our little angel. All a newborn could wish for is the affection of her mother. It is Mama who feeds her, bathes her, positions her body ever so carefully in the bassinette to ensure a comfortable nap. Changing all the smelly, poopy diapers - no problem. It's obvious that the baby feels her mother's affection. Life is so peaceful, so loving, so happy. Then the unthinkable happens. Our sweet little baby evolves into the worse thing imaginable; she becomes a toddler.

Now there's a little monster running around your house, writing on the walls, throwing food, falling out, pouring baby powder all on your couch. (Lol. Sorry for the flash-backs.) Before you know it, all the affection you once offered to your child has instantly metamorphosed into rage and frustration. What happened to your little angel? Where did she go? And who is this little she-devil? All jokes aside, how in the world can a mother show affection when all that is in front of her is bad behavior? The enemy has used our failure to properly raise our children, through training and discipline, to create a wall in the family. This is all because we, as mothers, have never really taught them how to behave.

Now, teaching a child how to behave is no walk in the park, believe me. However, it can be done. It will take instructions, rules, consequences, repercussions, reminders, encouragement, rewards and the main thing, patience. This list must be repeated over and over until they get it. It will take consistency on the parent's behalf. Again, I say, it can be done. Sadly, mothers today are not taking the time to teach, train and discipline their children so the poor children just don't know how to properly behave. Who should we really blame?

***Discipline your son, and he will give you peace; he will bring delight to your soul. Proverbs 29:17***

So, now we have a mother with an unruly child. As the child acts up and the mother yells and screams in frustration. She runs herself ragged reacting to her child's lack of self-control instead of teaching self-control. Now, Mama has no desire or energy for true affection, other than the affection that her belt has for the child's rear end. In this case, spankings are even un-affective. This dysfunctional interaction continues on and on until it becomes the only form of affection that the mother shows toward her child. As you can see, our children need our training early on, in order to make plenty of room for our affection, down the road.

So how do you relate this to raising teenagers? We, as mothers, can love on them all day when they are babies but when they grow older, the hugs and kisses are "few and far between." Many mothers think after her child reaches a certain age, (keep in mind I said "child"), that affection is no longer needed. If she tries to offer affection from time to time, the child begins to act totally embarrassed upon the slightest form of affection because he or she is not use to getting it.

When the adolescent years spring up on you, many mothers let go. Believe me, it's good to trust your child enough to give them a little rope but we, as mothers, shouldn't completely let go of the rope. When they try to act grown and try to convince you they don't need you or your "affection" so heavily in their lives, just remember that you are still MAMA! If you don't let them forget it then they won't. Believe me, they want you to show you care, every child does. Besides, if they were that grown, they wouldn't be still living in your house. So if you take an urge to haul off and hug them, then go right ahead. Kiss 'em while you're at it. Brag on them to your friends. Tell them you're proud of them. Grab their hand when you're walking together. Simply put, don't half-step with the motherly affection.

Now, I know that we have to be Mama. We have to crack the whip. We have to establish the rules. We have to set and enforce the expectations. Yes, we have to wear the combat boots. On the contrary, as a mother, it is often through our affection that we truly throw the lifeline to our children. As mothers, it is our responsibility to really "take care" of our children and by that I mean teach them, correct them, and especially love them. It's one thing to tell a person that you love them, but it's more important to show it. We show our love when we do things for people that reach their hearts. When someone hugs me, I feel affection.

When someone compliments me and brags on me, I feel affection. When someone truly shows concern for me and my interests and my dreams, I feel loving affection. These are all ways to show affection for our children. It is in a mother that our children seek these things. It's ok coming from someone else, but it is eternal when it comes from Mama.

Now for some mothers, we may have allowed the stress and pressure of simply providing the necessities for our children to take precedence over the need to show affection. I understand how that can easily happen. My goodness, when you are a mother with no parental support system, you may not have any energy left for the warm and fuzzy affection. However, each time we show the simplest act of affection toward our children, it's huge to them and our children feel our love. When they don't show that they appreciate our affection, in many cases it's simply because they are more accustomed to our harshness. They have to learn how to receive our affection. It really means the world to them, but when they are not used to our affection, it will be more uncomfortable for them to receive. This may cause rejection and when the children reject the mother, in many cases, the mother stops. This is, yet, another trick of the enemy and it's time we stop letting the devil kill the flow of affection in our families.

We have to understand that if we show affection to our children, it makes them happier, calmer and more confident. We should not under-estimate the importance of a little affection. Just a little hug when they slip and fall, even when you want to say, *"See, that's what your little behind gets for running in this house."* Mothers, we should show that we understand what they are going through. Encourage them, compliment them, sing their praises. The term, "Mama's boy" should go for girls, too. Not in a negative, childish way, but in a way to motivate our children. In a, *"If no one else believes in me, I know my Mama does,"* kind of way. This is a gift that a child is blessed to have from his or her mother. The belief in them that Mama has is enough to push a child straight to success.

A mother's affection—now that instantly sounds warm and snuggly, safe and protected, confident and prepared. Prepared for life; prepared for whatever obstacles or challenges may come their way. That child could conquer the world behind a good helping of a mother's affection. It picks you up and lifts you higher. It makes those around you know that you are loved. It proves your importance, making no need for you to search for more.

Now considering all the positive outcomes that will come from a mother who shows affection every chance she gets, imagine the life of the child whose mother has chosen to half-step. Imagine all the missed opportunities to show affection that have been replaced with a void. The void could be sadness or anger or jealously or rebellion. The reality is that something, and in some cases, someone will fill that void. Is there a void in your child's life? Who or what is filling that void? Scary, when you really think about it.

Wouldn't it be better for mothers to prevent these voids? If the void has already been established, reactively speaking, shouldn't we be the one to correct the problem and fill the voids in the lives of our children? This could decrease the chances of our daughters and sons getting into all types of trouble. When the time is right, then let these young girls find love and these boys find belonging and respect outside the home. Right now, they are not adults and they live under your roof and your job is to give them the affection they need. Let our children be children who love their mothers. Mothers, please love them back!

I know someone may be saying, *"I do love my children, I just don't have time to be "nice" all the time. I have to stay on my kids."* Well, I never said don't stay on them, but one does not replace the other. Both affection and discipline is needed. Just like with the flower we grew, we gotta have them both.

There are so many children dealing with problems that stemmed from a lack of affection. When you think about people who commit violent crimes, what do you think is the root of the hurt they have carried for so long? Yes, they are hurt. Some may call them evil or monsters but they are just people like you and I who have been severely hurt along the way. They, in turn, hurt other people. In comparison, I wonder how many of them received affection from their mothers and how many only received abuse. To commit a violent crime, one must have an *"I don't care about anything,"* attitude. They couldn't care about hurting someone or going to prison. They must be to the point of no return, with nothing to lose. Their hearts must be so far from peace and happiness that hurting someone else is the only way to release their own hurt. If they received the loving-kindness from their mothers, maybe they would have found the fulfillment for which they were searching. Maybe the void would have never taken root and grown into such rage. I know every violent crime perpetrator may not have been starving for a mother's affection, but what if your child is? What if your tender touch could change the path of destruction in your child's future? What if?

There are many women out there who are the mothers of serial killers, rapists, terrorists and even worse. For them, the damage is done. These mothers may feel that it is too late. But I say, for you and me, for us, for the women of our book clubs, for the members of your small groups, for each individual mother who reads the words printed on this page, for us, standing united against this spiritual warfare among our families and against our children, I say to you, it's not too late. We are right on time. God has prepared us for such a time as this. Mothers, don't half-step, show affection toward your children, that they might live. Show motherly love, that we all might raise our children and live in perfect peace. Feed their spirits with your affection. Can't you see they are starving? Feed them, mothers, feed them.

*"Jesus said, "Feed my lambs." John 21:15b*

# Sister Young's Way

AFFECTION WAS A WORD, with which, a person like Sister Young was very comfortable. She could show a bum off the street affection and not think twice. That was just her way. When she would come to the children's schools, her arms would be filled with all of her children's friends who stampeded her with hugs. She never responded as though the children overwhelmed or irritated her. She took the time to show affection toward anyone who needed it. Even a stranger would leave her presence feeling happy and loved. On the contrary, imagine what a lonely child's life would have become as a product of a mother like Sister Young. Imagine what it would have been like in her home. Let's look into the archives of her son's memory and get a glimpse of her affection.

Her youngest son, Corey, was very unique. There's always one out the bunch, who is just plain, ole gifted. Well, that was Corey. If you showed him something once, he perfected it. He was a brilliant scholar, making straight A's and he was also a talented musician. After Mama's own heart, he too, played piano. He had lots of potential and Sister Young's only concern was that he lived up to that potential. So, she kept him busy. She made sure Corey took advantage of all opportunities out there. Since Corey was such a quick learner, he didn't require as much of his mother's attention on a daily basis compared to some other siblings. However, Sister Young was always present when he really needed her and because of that, he reported that he never felt neglected by her. Never. There was one instance where Sister Young's affection toward Corey branded his heart forever.

Corey was attending Springdale Elementary at the time and, of course, he was chosen to compete in the big Spelling Bee. This contest would take him to the regional Spelling Bee at Snowden Elementary and then to the City-wide Competition. Everyone had high hopes that Corey would reign victorious and go all the way. Surprisingly to all, the unthinkable happened. Corey misspelled the word biscuit. He spelled it b-i-s-c-u-t. It was a tremendous disappointment to many, but to Corey, it was devastating. After the contest, he returned to class sad and embarrassed. His teacher, acknowledging his loss, allowed Corey to lay his head down on his desk and excused him from the remaining day's class work.

Finally, Corey made it home from this awful day in his young life. After what he experienced, it would be nice to come home to a safe haven of comfort and peace. Fortunately for him, Sister Young stopped what she was doing and gave all her attention and affection toward her dear son Corey. She did not throw salt on an open wound by making him re-live the tragic moment with comments and questions that only would have made matters worse. Many mothers may have asked, *"How did you miss that easy word?"* Sister Young, however, simply rubbed her son's back as he cried himself to sleep. Corey's response to that memory was, *"I know my Mama loved me that day."* Sister Young made it a point to teach her children how to show affection. As I mentioned earlier, she taught the boys how to treat a lady and required them to practice on her and their sisters. What is more affectionate to a woman than to be in the presence of a real gentleman? She partnered the children, one boy with one girl, and the boys' responsibilities were to always look after their designated sister. If a man grows to learn how to look after his sister, he will understand what it means to look after his wife and family. Sister Young also showed affection openly to her beloved husband, Brother Ben.

As we know, Sister Young did not hold back on the guidance, nurturing, training, and discipline. Consequently, since her children were well trained and had learned how to behave, it was easier for her to show affection toward them. Mothers, do you see the pattern here? Do you see how one life lesson leads to the next? She still had to get on them and some more than others. Yet and still, had it not been for the affection of Sister

Young, her children and so many others would not have emotionally become what they are today. The affection that Sister Young showed as a mother was appreciated and definitely needed.

Discussion:

- Identify and discuss ways to show affection toward children of various ages.
- What is your personal scripture of promise that addresses the need to show affection toward your child(ren)?

# Chapter #6 – Love

IN THIS CHAPTER, WE will talk about the word, "LOVE". This word can sum up all the five proceeding chapters in this book. Without love, God's love might I add, a mother cannot effectively execute nurturing, guidance, training, discipline, or affection. Yet, this word has been abused, used lightly, and interpreted in many ways. We call it tough love, puppy love, love–hate, and the list goes on and on. However, love is simple; we make it complicated. If there is any un-comfort or resistance, we allow our love to waiver. Could it be that we haven't truly understood how unconditional God's love for us really is? Without God's love, how can we truly have motherly love? We have created our own variations of love which validates our poor respect for love. So, before we go any further, let us examine the biblical definition of love.

> *"⁴Love is patient, love is kind. It does not envy, it does not boast, it is not proud. ⁵ It does not dishonor others, it is not self-seeking, it is not easily angered, it keeps no record of wrongs. ⁶ Love does not delight in evil but rejoices*

**with the truth. ⁷ It always protects, always trusts, always hopes, always perseveres. ⁸Love never fails." I Corinthians 13:4-8a**

As we come to the final step in restoring our plant, the reason for it all was love. It was our love that led us to provide nurture and affection when we rescued our plant and made the decision to restore it back to health. It was our love that led us to offer guidance and training with our stick. Our love inspired us to take the time to discipline the plant, by pulling up the weeds. It was our love that led us to show it off to our friends.

After each and every act of love that was needed, now look at our plant. Do you see what I see? We now have a plant that is so beautiful, so healthy, so stable and strong. Let's just take a moment to appreciate the life of this beautiful plant that we saved. Because of love, unselfish love, our plant has survived. This love is wonderful.

My plant may not have the leaves in the same places as yours. The big, colorful petals of its bulb may not be positioned just as yours. So what? It's mine and I love it. I love this beautiful being that will brighten my day and bring joy to my soul. I love yours, as well. I also love yours and yours and yours, too. Yes, mothers, you guessed it. I'm really talking about our children.

Saving this plant is simply a metaphor, illustrating the need to save our children.

Oh, but wait, what's that smell? Fresh, like rain. The sky has become dark. There are loud explosions of lightning and thunder. Oh no, what about our beautiful flower? We can't let the thunderstorm ruin it again. This is no time to half-step. We can't just sit back and do nothing, as if our job here is ever complete. What we must do may require us to get our hair wet, but oh well. In this step, we must *rescue the flower again, and repeat all five steps, over and over again, whenever needed.*

From the first moment a mother finds out she is pregnant, the love is immediately established. Yes, there are unwanted pregnancies that bring fear, shame, guilt and other emotions that may suppress a mother's love for her unborn child. However, as the child grows and begins to move around in a mother's stomach, in most cases, the love grows stronger. All the pain, discomfort, and did I mention, pain, that a mother experiences from conception until birth only increases the love. So when our children make mistakes along the path of life, a "real mother" is not so quick to leave her children out to dry. There's a bond between a mother and her child that keeps Mama's feet planted firmly. This bond is deep and sometimes unexplainable. This bond between a mother and her child is rooted in love.

For our plant, it was love that tugged at your heart to rescue it. Your love has grown because you watched this flower grow from a fragile, near death situation to the beautiful existence that is shown now. Yes, you did love it when it was unattractive and that was why you restored it. In comparison, it is the same love that has struck in us a desire to do better as mothers.

Now, for mothers who feel they are lacking in the area of love, or they just don't know where to begin, let's start by re-evaluating our love for God.

*"He answered, 'Love the Lord your God with all your heart and with all your soul and with all your strength and with all your mind'; and, 'Love your neighbor as yourself.'" Luke 10:27*

If we love God with all that we have and consider our loved ones as we consider ourselves, then we can better meet the needs of our children. It is also written,

*"If you love me, keep my commands." John 14:15*

It is much easier to live a happy, joyous life when you are not burdened by the guilt of sin. If we truly love God as He is requiring us to, then we would put forth a more consistent and determined effort to keep His commands. When a person knows that he or she is living in obedience to God, that person's self-respect is strengthened. I can love myself if I respect myself. I can respect myself if I am not living under the restraints of guilt and shame. When we can openly love ourselves, we can openly love our children.

There are mothers out there who claim that they "love" their children so deeply that they can't bring themselves to discipline them as we discussed in chapter 4. *"It just breaks my heart to have to spank my sweet little angel."* Ultimately, you are saying, *"I love you too much to raise you, even though I am your parent and it's my responsibility."* Meanwhile, the child becomes as spoiled as a month old carton of milk—just stinking up the place. Mothers, this won't work a minute longer.

The true essence of the word "love" led God the Father to send His only begotten son. Spanking your child could never compare to what God did; sending His only child to sacrifice His life and die for the sins of the whole world. Yes, this is the single word that will convince a half-stepping mother to examine herself and step up her game—love.

So, tell me, how long can we continue to behave in the same manner and proclaim we love our children? We all know the definition of insanity, right? If we expect something different, we must do something differently. Our children need their mothers and that alone should be our motivation to make sure we are in place. We should make sure we give them the love they so desperately need.

How can a heavy built man impose all his force to beat his petite, feeble wife and say he loves her? How can that be? How can teachers and ministers secretly have sexual relations with children and say they love them? Don't ask me, I can't understand it. I don't know why people mistreat animals or why Assistant Living professionals mistreat our elderly. I couldn't begin to explain the mind-set of criminals, or of killers, or of rapists. All I know, love has very little to do with it. If I say, "I love you," then how can I hurt you? How can I? Mothers, how can we? Yet, every time we miss another opportunity to show our love toward our children, it is them that we truly hurt.

So when you close this book and your child walks in the house from school, love him. During the next phone conversation, text message or email, love him. If you are friends on Facebook, update your status and proclaim your love for your child. I know love is better shown, not spoken; nonetheless, we are going to start by telling them. Some of us haven't told them in a very long time. We may even owe them an apology for taking so long to tell them. It doesn't matter, though.

We are starting this relationship on a brand new slate. This time, we will not half-step.

A mother's love is that of protection, provision, and purity. It never lets up, it never gets tired and it never ends. Imagine a young toddler who recently learned to crawl. The toddler is on the loose and is headed for a table, on which lies a burning candle. There is also a cup of hot coffee in the curious baby's reach. A mother's first response is to quickly grab the baby, right? A mother's love will direct her to look out for the safety of this beloved, helpless child. A mother's love would know that it would have only been a natural instinct for the toddler to reach for the candle or knock over the hot coffee. A mother's love would have questioned herself, as to why these things were in the child's reach to begin with. Why is it that these same examples of love are suppressed once the toddler reaches a certain age? For these same reasons, we should re-evaluate our place in our children's lives. We must reinforce our children's assurance in knowing that Mama is there for them, just like when they were toddlers. (Figuratively speaking, you know what I mean.) Our children should feel our love for them by knowing that in any situation, Mama is going to be there to grab them back to safety, not to spoil them or stunt their growth and maturity, but to support and empower them.

# Sister Young's Way

For many mothers, its very hard to show love. All they know is "tough love". Tough love is fine when there is a need for it, but sometimes a child just needs a plain, old hug from Mama; just to know he is loved and supported. Well, Sister Young had no problems in this category.

Keep in mind, she did have six children, remember? She had to balance her love and affection between them all, in addition to, her husband and the many, many other friends and family who were consistently pulling on her. People were always turning to Sister Young for a dose of love, because she always came through for them. Her heart was so big, she really did have enough love to go around. However, regarding her children, she made it her priority to ensure that each of them was emotionally and affectionately sound. None of them felt lost in the crowd.

One thing that is often missing today, Sister Young openly showed love for her husband, in front of the children. Brother Ben was not a "hopeless romantic" husband, as he was more of a serious, no-nonsense type of person. Nonetheless, the children remembered their mother chasing their father around the house trying to steal a kiss and oh, how the children would laugh. She didn't use Brother Ben's lack of affection toward her as a platform to fight or be upset with him. Instead, she decided to show her love for her husband, regardless. There must be submission to show affection toward someone who may or may not do the same in return. It doesn't seem fair if you view it through natural eyes. However, Sister Young viewed things through spiritual eyes and the Word of God taught her.

Imagine how many lost marriages could have been spared if they really understood the verse about wives submitting to their husbands the ways Sister Young did. Sister Young didn't expect things to revolve around her. She made you feel that it was her pleasure to be in your presence. How beautiful to be a person like Sister Young—so loving. She was there for her husband and her children and not the other way around. It was about them and not her.

Sister Young knew all about this word love. She was this word. Her entire being described this word. She showed those around her how to love through Christ Jesus. Yes, she loved so many and so many loved her right back, but let's look deeper at her motherly love.

Kia remembered one of her first real heartbreaks. We all remember our first heartbreak and it was no laughing matter. Despite her sadness, Kia remembered being teased about it. *"Someone your age knows nothing about love. That's puppy love."* How about that for kicking her when she was down? Oh, but Sister Young knew how to shed light into a conversation. She simply replied to that puppy love wise-crack, *"….it's real to the puppies"*. She would have never undermined Kia's feelings at a time like that—no way.

> **"Let no one despise your youth, but be an example to the believers in word, in conduct, in love, in spirit, in faith, in purity." I Timothy 4:12**

Kia even had warm memories of her mother during a particular time when the Young household was very different from the rest. There was a time when they did not have a single TV in the house. Brother Ben called the TV a *"one*-eyed devil". Imagine what his opinion of TV would be now. Anyway, during that time, the children did a lot of reading, playing outdoors, taking care of their chores or studies, practicing their individual extra-curricular activities, but most of all, they spent time together and had a lot of fun. Nonetheless, the fact remained that there were certain TV shows that all kids just wanted to see. Their friends at school probably talked about some of those shows the next day at school. Realistically, no one wanted to be left out of those conversations because you didn't have a TV at home. We all remember the first few seasons of Cosby. No one missed a single episode. Well, Sister Young understood that and she showed empathy regarding things that made her children happy. Even though Brother Ben did not buy them another TV, Kia remembered her mother allowing her to go down to a neighbors house to watch "What's Happening" and sometimes Kia could even convince Sister Young to come along, too. Why, because she loved her daughter and she wasn't so strict that she couldn't bend a little.

### *Delight yourself also in the Lord and He will give you the desires of your heart" Psalm 37:4*

One of the biggest examples of Sister Young's love for her children was when she left her career to raise them full time. During the late 60's / early 70's, things were not as easily attainable for American Americans as they are today. For Sister Young, being said to be the first black chemist in Memphis was ground breaking. She had it going on. With her intelligence and her winning personality, she had a bright future ahead of her. As she weighed career in one hand and family in the other, there was no comparison for Sister Young. It was not a hard decision to make either. In the archives of her employee record at Buckman Laboratories, it reads: Reason for Resignation: TO BE A FULL TIME

HOMEMAKER. Now that's love. Wait a minute—let me go back further than this.

Sister Young had rough pregnancies. She stayed sick and sometimes she was bed-written during her final trimesters. God was showing her right there that her place was not in an office. She was to begin the nurturing process while her child was yet in her wound. She was to rest and take care of herself and her unborn child. Many mothers today get their tubes tied after the first rough pregnancy but not Sister Young. She always endured, with her eye on the prize. Her new baby was always the prize.

She loved God first, she did not despise her responsibilities as a mother of six, and she truly loved motherhood. When you love something, you give it your all. You give it your best, without murmuring and complaining, in spite of frustrations and impatience. You appreciate the fact that God has blessed you to have something you love. It becomes your pleasure in life. You put yourself into it and if greatness is within you, it will show in that which you love. Greatness was within Sister Young and it showed in her children.

Until this day, her greatness shows in her children. Her oldest two, Joy and Steve were the first to get married and to begin families of their own. Astonishing to believe, the other four siblings decided since they were not yet married, why not buy a big home and live together? Most families today couldn't spend a weekend under the same roof without arguing, fighting, disrespecting each other and so on. None of this foolishness exists in the Young family. They were so close that they could actually live together in harmony. That speaks volumes.

Since then, Kia entered holy matrimony and has also become a mother. Corey has also married and is now a father. (Corey got married on his parent's wedding anniversary.) Camille is happily engaged and Kevin is still the world most eligible bachelor. Lol.

You can see a little of Sister Young in each of them. Compassion, a listening ear, encouragement, help, intellect, college degrees, talent, generosity, beauty, charisma, I could really go on and on. These are things you find in all six of her children. Most of all, in her children she left the best legacy of all, a life-long love for God.

---

Discussion:
- Identify and discuss ways to show love for children of various ages.
- What is your personal scripture of promise that addresses the need to show love toward your child(ren)?

# The Life Conclusion
## of Sister Young

## As a Christian

God wants His people to be fruitful and multiply. We know that Sister Young understood the multiply part, but let's look at how she was fruitful. If we examined each, "fruit of the spirit," as described in Ephesians and compared it to Sister Young's life, we identify the following:

- Joy – Laughter is an element of happiness and joy; ergo, Sister Young's laughter and her winning smile signified her inner joy. She counted it joy to raise her children and spend time with them. It brought her joy to help people and show God's love.
- Peace – Sister Young never complained about her situations or responsibilities. It was un-

common for her to show heavy stress or worry. It was unusual for her to yell or scream around the house, as she was slow to anger. God gave her peace within herself and it showed.

- Longsuffering – In light of Sister Young's lack of wealth, the sacrifice of her professional career, and through her health complication, she kept her eyes on the prize. Her mission to be a good mother and a faithful Christian was her commitment in life. At all cost, she never strayed from this lifelong mission. People today allow things in life to destroy them; yet, Sister Young pressed her way through disappointments or misfortunes in life. She did it all with a smile.

- Kindness – As a mother, Sister Young never tore the children down. She was compassionate even when she had to discipline them. She always made time for people. Her personality made people happy and lifted their spirits. She was so nice.

- Goodness – We all remember as a child being reminded to, "Be a good girl, be a good boy". Who reminds us to be "good" when we become an adult? Sister Young truly possessed goodness. Not one single child can remember her acting in disobedience. She never gossiped or argued with friends and family. She was honest in her actions and her ethics. She practiced what she preached.

- Faithfulness – She was faithful to all her children. They never felt neglected. She spent private time with each one of them and supported them all. Her faithfulness as a wife showed both in her marriage, as well as, in her faithfulness to support Brother Ben in his ministry. She was also faithful and confidential as a friend.

- Gentleness – She was compassionate, understanding, and approachable. She often hugged and kissed her family and friends. She approached and resolved conflict gently with soft spoken words.

- Self-Control - She did not overspend money. She was prudent and she taught the children how to live a disciplined life. She knew when to be professional and when to keep it real; when to be funny and when to be serious. She always controlled her anger. She did not pour all of her time and attention into one particular thing. She had balance.

So, if someone out there was wondering if Sister Young half-stepped as a Christian, I think not. I believe she received that crown in heaven. (Remember the earthly crown that she so modestly declined to accept at her Love Day Appreciation?) I believe she finally earned that crown with many, many jewels. So for all of the wealth and possessions she may have sacrificed here on earth, I would say she received 100 fold in heaven. (Bling-bling, Sister Young. Bling-bling eternally.)

So, as I look over my notes from each chapter of this book that I have taken from Sister Young's life story as a mother, the list of her key best practices would be:

- Take the time to **nurture** and show support
- Offer **guidance** both spiritual and common sense
- **Train** the children with authority, using both the rod and compassion
- Teach self-**discipline** while making it fun / **discipline** and correct them consistently
- Expose the children to loving **affection**
- Show and prove your **love**, beyond a shadow of a doubt

I still believe that it was greatly because of Sister Young's strong devotion to her faith that she possessed the integrity and character which made her who she was. After looking at so many examples of her as a mother, now I want to celebrate the content of her character as a Christian.

Many of us, as Christians, pick and choose what we trust God for. We say that God can do anything but fail. We go to church, sing and wave our hands in praise and worship. However, when the rubber meets the road and we are faced with some of the tougher challenges in life, many of us simply do not have the faith that is needed for God to perform magnificent miracles that are in His divine power. Now, do you think a person like Sister Young would have been a vessel for God to perform a miracle? Do you think her faith would have been strong enough to show the world God's most awesome power? If put in a situation that requires a belief in God to do something you have never seen Him do for anyone else, do you think Sister Young would have stood on God's promises or would she fold under pressure? Considering all that I have already told you about the special anointing that Sister Young had, we shouldn't be surprised or reluctant to imagine that her faith was suitable to be used by God to perform the impossible, move the unmoveable, capture the intangible, and receive the unbelievable power of the Lord our God.

You see, Sister Young battled breast cancer. When I say, "battled," I truly mean just that. The best part about it, she fought her cancer and she won. Now, I am not judging anyone who uses any methods other than what Sister Young chose and if I were in her shoes, God only knows what I, myself, would do. I cannot honestly say I would have the courage to rise to the occasion as Sister Young did. All I can say is, I highly admire her for what I am about to tell you.

Sister Young prayed to God for a spiritual and natural approach toward treatment and healing of this disease. Her faith in God's Word was incredibly strong and she did not waiver. According to the Word, God is a healer. If the Word said God could heal her, then Sister Young was crazy enough to believe it. Why not? Instead of standing on His promises, we take matters into our own hands and, in many cases, we make matters worse. Not Sister Young. When she received her diagnosis of cancer, she marched right over to her spiritual friend and confidant, who happened to be an expert on natural health and healing, Brother Franco Taylor, Master Herbalist and International Health Educator for *Right Stuff Health Systems* of Memphis, TN.

When she first told Brother Franco about the situation of the cancer, she was very gentle in sharing this news with him. It was almost like she wanted to protect his feelings of fear on her behalf. This was the type of person she was: always concerned with the feelings of others. So after carefully breaking it to him, she asked his opinion regarding natural healing. Brother Franco first offered a word of prayer and then he took her to the Word of God.

*"If you diligently heed the voice of the Lord your God and do what is right in His sight, give ear to His commandments and keep all His statutes, I will put <u>none</u> of the diseases on you which I have brought on the Egyptians. "For I am the Lord who heals you." Exodus 15:26*

This scripture was the answer to this question, "Will this work?" God said He would put **none** of the diseases on the righteous. That included cancer. This verified to her that healing was possible. Then Brother Franco took her to:

*"Along the bank of the river, on this side and that, will grow all kinds of trees used for food; their leaves will not wither, and their fruit will not fail. They will bear fruit every month, because their water flows from the sanctuary. Their fruit will be for food and their leaves for medicine." Ezekiel 47:12*

This verified that healing agents was naturally found in the foods we eat. He also referenced the vision given to John in Revelations 22:2 about the leaves of the tree of life being used for the healing of the nations. In the beginning, (in the book of Genesis), God gave fruits, nut, grains, and vegetables that were to keep Adam and Eve alive forever.

Applying the truths of the Word of God was the basis of the type of faith Sister Young had. Seeking directions from the scriptures, through the man of God and her dear friend Brother Franco, was the obvious approach for Sister Young. Brother Franco referred to scripture, considering how in the beginning, God gave fruits, nuts, grains, and vegetables that were to keep them alive forever. So Brother Franco helped Sister Young create a healing regiment for her treatment, which specifically involved her diet and exercise. I'm sure you're not surprised to hear that Sister Young followed it to a tee.

The goal was to boost her immune system. Brother Franco explained that her natural immunity could be boosted to its highest force, through the consumption of the most nutritious raw fruits, vegetables and lean meats. In doing this, Sister Young's immune system would have the capability to reject the cancer from her body. Now, Sister Young had to totally commit to this new way of eating. During the course of this process, Sister Young's skin became extremely clear and pretty. There was a beautiful glow about her. She looked very, very good.

Some of the things that I have learned about Sister Young have seemed to be surreal. How could a person stand on God's Word so firmly? Sister Young prayed to God to heal her of this ugly, deadly sickness and she stood on her faith that He would. Without the use of conventional methods of therapy, she turned to scripture for natural and spiritual measures of treatment. Now this, my friend, is an example of a modern day woman of faith who was determined to touch the hem of His garment. (You know what I mean?)

Now, I must tell you that the children remembered the bloody gals. They remember helping her dress the open wound that developed in her breast, as the healing began to take its course. They remembered how weak she was and how much she suffered through the healing process. Her faith in God's healing power was the ammunition needed for Sister Young to endure the pain. All the while, she continued her responsibilities as First Lady of the church and as City-Wide President of the Memphis PTA. Sister Young, as we see, fought her cancer head on. She didn't use her sickness as a crutch at all. She kept going just as if nothing was even wrong, until the pains hit. She would then stop, bear the pain, and keep moving.

During this tedious time for her, she yet supported the children in all of their involvements. Her middle daughter Kia was a very skilled basketball player. We all want to look in the stands and see our wonderful mother cheering us on to victory. Well, Kia certainly knew what that felt like. Sister Young's breast may have been bleeding and she may have been weak in pain, but when Kia turned and looked in the stands, she saw her loving mother smiling right back at her. For Sister Young, it wasn't about herself, it was about her children.

How many of us would be looking for a reason to not be involved in something with our children? Some parents have never been to their children's sports games or performances. Why? Are we too lazy, too selfish, too uninterested? Half-steppers, if this describes you then own it, because there are some major changes that must be made.

Sister Young continued to meet all her children needs. That's just how she was, a helper to many, always denying herself for the greater good of her fellow man. She didn't have time for any pity parties. She had a responsibility to her God, her husband, her children and even her community. She touched so many, she influenced so many, and she inspired so many, and still, even until today.

Sister Young brought new meaning to the spiritual fruit, "long-suffering". In all things, she gave thanks. In all things, she delighted in the Lord. Bringing glory to God was her motivation. She had no reason to be sad or worried, complaining, "woe is me." She always knew that she was never alone. She always knew that God was with her.

**"I will never leave you nor forsake you." Hebrews 13:5**

So how do you think this story ended? Remarkable, through the pain, through this cross that she bore, through her longsuffering—the cancer literally exited through her breast. Yes, you heard me right. **The cancer surfaced through an open wound and came out of Sister Young's breast.** Can you even remotely imagine that? This is mind-boggling; absolutely astonishing to me. The cancer came through her breast and she was healed. No medicine, no chemo, and no radiation. Can anyone who does not believe in God's power please explain this? I didn't think so. God promised to work with those of us who have a mustard seed of faith, so imagine the miracles God can perform in the lives of people with faith like Sister Young's.

**"Truly I tell you, if you have faith as small as a mustard seed, you can say to this mountain, 'Move from here to there,' and it will move. Nothing will be impossible for you." Matthew 17:20**

We have to know that God still heals. We have to know this, without a shadow of doubt. All of this to say, God's order equals life. Man's order, independent from God's guidance, could very well lead to death and we don't even know it.

Sister Young was purposed to prove God's power. God healed her of cancer because of her faith and obedience. The same way He healed Sister Young's sickness, He can heal the sickness that exists in motherhood today. We have to seek spiritual healing the same way Sister Young sought physical healing and that is in the Word of God. Just like Sister Young, we must suffer through the pain of the process. We must continuously seek God through prayer, maintaining a healthy lifestyle before our children. That means we may have to change some stuff in our lives. Sister Young had to change some eating habits, didn't she? She wasn't feeding her body the right stuff. Well, we are not feeding our spirits the right stuff, nor the spirits of our children.

As a mother, there are some things we need to do more, differently, and better. So yes, we do need to change some habits in order for this thing to work. Our faith, (just like Sister Young immune system), must be increased. It needs a serious boost in order to carry us into the healing of our broken families. We must remember to keep our eyes on the prize, even though it may hurt sometimes. It may seem hopeless. It may seem easier to just give up. However, if we just hold on and believe what God promised us, God will show Himself mightily, right before our eyes. Generational curses will be broken, relationships will be restored and our children will be saved. God is waiting on us to let Him. Just try and see; you won't be disappointed.

> *"O taste and see that the LORD is good: blessed is the man that trusts in him." Psalm 34:8*

How can we allow God to perform miracles in our lives without putting ourselves in our most vulnerable place and saying, *"Yes, oh Lord, I will trust you. I don't see any way out of this, but I'm going to trust you with it all."* So I say to each and every mother (or father); don't dwell on the mistakes you've made in the past. Get up, dust yourself off, and put all of your energy in making things better with you and your children. Have faith that God can and will restore that which is broken. With that faith, walk into your future. It was Sister Young's faith that led her to her healing. With that faith, watch God heal your family and save your children.

> **"Be of good cheer, daughter; your faith has made you well." Matthew 9:22**

# As a Fisher of Men

WELL, AS WE COME to the conclusion of all the wonderful memories found through the life of Sister Young, there is one thing that we can say Sister Young did not do. She did not half-step. Oh no, she loved like it was going out of style. Even in the mist of her battle with cancer, she never half-stepped. News Flash: When it's all over, there will be no time to go back and do things you should have done or say things you should have said. We have to savor the moment and take advantage of today's opportunities to teach, support, and be a good example for our children. Sister Young certainly did.

Sister Young was absolutely loved by everyone who knew her. The church folks loved her, the school system loved her, the neighborhood loved her, the City of Memphis loved her. Everyone loved her because she loved them. It was not fake; it was real. It was genuine. Through her, God's love was felt and shared.

Her middle son Kevin remembered an example of how her love and protection saved him from a seriously dangerous situation. One day, he remembered running home from school in fear of a group of kids who had threatened to jump him. In fear for his safety, he told his mother what was about to happen. Sister Young, of course, intervened and told Kevin to go inside so she could talk to the group of boys. The loving kindness that she showed toward the group of children made it impossible for them to disrespect her. To this day, no one will ever know what Sister Young actually said to them to calm the situation. Whatever it was, it was said in love. The kids left in peace and they never bothered Kevin again.

The anointing of God equals power. Sister Young knew how to bring peace to chaos because her voice, her words, her personality exuded peace.

### *"A soft answer turns away wrath, but a harsh word stirs up anger." Proverb 15:1*

She was the type of person who was confident and equipped to handle any circumstance. She could laugh and cut up with the country folks one minute and then engage in stimulating conversation with the intellectuals the very next minute. She could hang with the best or the worse of them and never make anyone feel uncomfortable. You could always depend on Sister Young to provide you with just the hug or smile or prayer or encouraging words your heart needed.

We applaud her diligence and persistence in handling things as a mother should. There's no denying that Sister Young was a great mother, but she was so much more. Her capacity level to share motherly love far surpassed her six children. Her energy was more than most people could imagine having. So many people describe her as being full of life. The problem we see today, most people are lifeless. They are lazy beyond compare. How could Sister Young ever enjoy a lazy moment when she was constantly involved in so much? From running around with all of the children and each of their extra activities, to handling the church affairs; she stayed on the run morning, noon, and night. Not to mention her involvement with the NAACP, City Wide PTA President, local PTA President, Board of Directors for Mission Possible, Neighborhood Christian Center volunteer, Memphis Urban League volunteer, the U.S. Census volunteer, advisor for various women's retreats in the area and more and more and much, much more.

### *"...faith without works is dead." James 2:20*

Many children today are not given the opportunity to participate in activities because their parents won't commit to taking them to and from practices. It was described by one of her friends that Sister Young kept her children involved in many activities in her effort to build her children's character. If that was her motive, then #1, it worked and #2, sacrificing her lazy time to run around for her children was a small price to pay. The half-steppers of today have no desire to sacrifice a moment of their lazy time for anyone including their own children.

If only more people, especially Christians, could be more like Sister Young, as a helper of mankind and a selfless giver of one's self. If people became more considerate of others, then there would be less road rage accidents, because people would be more courteous drivers, who know how to take turns, merge, and slow things down. Many of us can't even remember the last time we drove our cars slowly and enjoyed the scenery. Stopping to help someone in distress is certainly too much to ask. Sister Young would sometimes run late for engagements simply because she did enjoy the scenery and she did stop to help people in distress.

There would be fewer arguments because no one would dare say anything to deliberately offend another. Can that really be done? Sister Young did it. There would be fewer fights because one would never raise their hand to strike any human being. Sister Young didn't. There would be fewer murders because there would never have been a fight to begin with. Sister Young never fought, well, other than with her brother when they were little. Anyway, you get my point.

**"And let us consider one another in order to stir up love and good works." Hebrews 10:24**

Overall, Sister Young stood for patience. She had patience for people who did not know any better. Those who were considered unlearned; those who have dwelled in darkness. She understood that people in darkness were expected to act like the darkness. That is why her light shined so brightly. It was a light of compassion; a light of patience. Instead of being angered by the actions of certain people, she saw the reason behind their actions and she reacted with mercy.

> *"Brethren, if a man is overtaken in any trespass, you who are spiritual restore such a one in a spirit of gentleness, considering yourself lest you also be tempted. Galatians 6:1*

She never blamed the person for his indiscretions, but she gave them hope that God could lift them to a higher place. If anyone could get through to you, Sister Young could. Her words were never to scold you, always to uplift and encourage you. The wind beneath your wings, she was. She was the very beacon of hope for those who needed it most. Even during your first encounter with her, it was like she had always known you and she was in it with you. She felt your pain with you during your sadness and she truly rejoiced with you during your time of celebration. She was your personal cheerleader, whether she'd known you ten years or ten minutes.

When you think about a, *"I put my neighbor before myself,"* type of love, I just wonder how many examples can most people look back over their lives and count. I wonder how many people can truly give examples of denying themselves. How many children can say their mother put them first? What about you?

In celebrating Sister Young's life, the word humanitarian came to mind. When I thought of all the many great people who have worked so diligently to change the conditions in the world, I saw Sister Young in that same light in her community, from a spiritual standpoint. Surprisingly, as I dug a little deeper into the true meaning of a humanitarian, I learned some definitions that changed my opinion, making it impossible to stamp this label of humanitarian on Sister Young's legacy. I realized that this title did not describe Sister Young at all.

Humanitarian n. One who believes that Christ was a mere man; an anti-Trinitarian. One who holds that the perfectibility of the human race is attainable without superhuman aid.

Oooooooh no! By definition, Sister Young stood for so much more. Now, it is not my intention to discredit anyone who has received this prestigious recognition as a humanitarian. However, when we talk about Sister Young and all the good that she did in her life, there is one big difference. Yes, her life was devoted to the greater good of people, as is many humanitarians. The difference is—Jesus Christ was the center of the whole operation. Her Lord and Savior was the focal point the entire way. She wasn't worried about being politically correct, so why is it such a concern of ours? The world uses the need to be politically correct, separating church from state, as a spiritual trick to steer us away from that which is Godly. The Bible teaches us that our fight is not against flesh and blood, but it is spiritual warfare. There is so much that happens right before our eyes that we allow and it is killing us. We accept anything and we stand for nothing. Sister Young stood for her faith and she wasn't ashamed of it. It was her faith that defined her and led her to the greatness that she achieved in her life. Humanitarian, she was not. Fisher of men, she was.

> ***"…follow me and I will make you
> fishers of men" Matthew 4:19***

After the victory of her healed breast cancer, similar to many cases, the cancer redeveloped. Through it all, she kept her spirits up, even until the end. When people would visit her in the hospital, instead of them bringing cheer and encouragement to her, she offered hope and encouragement to them. People would leave her hospital room uplifted. It was so incredible how positive she was.

During this time in the hospital, she maintained

her sense of humor and she would even crack jokes. Once when she was asked how her night had been, she gave a solemn, emotional reply, *"It was rough."* She then explained with a comical tone, *"Every time I finally fell asleep, Mama would wake me up to ask how I was feeling."* LOL! You see what I mean? She wanted everyone to be uplifted and never saddened by anything that God allowed to happen to her.

**"In every thing give thanks: for this is the will of God Christ Jesus concerning you." I Thessalonians 5:18**

When you think about it, there are a few things in life that are mandatory to live a healthy life such as food, water, exercise, etc. Do we all realize that prayer is one of those mandatory pieces of that puzzle? Well, if you don't know, you better ask somebody. It is very important that we understand the truest significance of the practice of prayer. You see, many mothers don't quite understand the power of prayer. Now my questions to the mothers, *"Are you praying for your children? Are you really praying for them?"*

Understanding the need and purpose of prayer is essential. We must all understand the power that lies in petitioning a spiritual covering over your children. We must understand that through prayer, God can break yokes and change the hearts and minds of our children.

There was a time when I took it lightly, prayer that is. I was the perfect example of the two minute, *"Lord, please bless my children, in the name of Jesus, thank you, bye."* My mother-in-law would often ask me, *"Heather, are you praying for the children? Are you praying for your husband?"* Of course, I would answer, *"Yes"* but in the back of my mind, I'm thinking, *"Why won't she stop pressuring me about praying? I pray!"* That was only my conscience rebelling simply because my prayers were truly without substance.

I'm not telling mothers to get the stop watches

and the timers out because the short prayers really should be a part of our day; several times a day. All I'm saying is, part of being a mother is sending up those purposed-filled petitions to the Father for coverage and direction for our children. When you've fussed all you can fuss, try prayer. When you've said all you know to say, try prayer. When you've paid all your money for private school and therapy, and extra activities and lessons to keep them out of trouble; try prayer. I say to you, begin praying for them regularly and see what happens. On the street they call it, "Putting in work." Mothers, I ask you to labor in prayer regularly. It's your responsibility, so don't half-step!

*Be anxious for nothing, but in everything,*
*by prayer and supplication, with*
*thanksgiving, lets your requests be made*
*known to God. Philippians 4:6*

When I think about Jesus on the cross, being beaten to death, like a run-away slave, with His last breath, He chose to pray to God, *"Father forgive them for they know not what they do."* Jesus already knew His destiny. He knew He would be crucified. He knew the calling on His life. So, after a beating like that, it was pretty obvious that those prophecies of his crucifixion were becoming a reality. If you knew that the end of your life was at hand, what would you do? What would you say? Would you pray? Who would you pray for? Some hypothetical questions are hard to answer. I don't know exactly what I would pray for during my last moments. Oh, but let me tell you about the last moments of the life of Sister Young.

In my interviews with the family, everyone often spoke of how spiritual Sister Young was and how she often labored in prayer for them. Yet, it was when I spoke to Mother Thomas, Sister Young's mother, that my spirit was truly touched by the essence of Sister Young's commitment to motherhood.

As I mentioned, the cancer had redeveloped. This time, Sister Young had become very ill and she was hospitalized. Mother Thomas remembered being there with her the night before she passed away. Perhaps Sister Young knew that the end of her journey was upon her. Nevertheless, with all the energy she had, she prayed for her children all night long. She prayed and prayed, calling out each of her six children's names, laboring in prayer while she could. While the blood was still running warm in her veins, Sister Young did the best thing a mother could do for her children, she prayed for them.

Sister Young did not spend her last moments in fear or pity for her own life. Her children were her focus, even until death. She knew that her children truly belonged to God. They were gifts given to her as a temporary stewardship. When God called Sister Young home, her faith gave her the confidence to know that her children would be in God's hands. This is why her dying deed was to pray for them. This story ends with a mother's prayer at its finest; the most eloquent example of a mother interceding for her children. She showed us to what extent a mother should put her children first: in her definition, until death. I do believe God received those prayers because until this day, all six of her children are well. Just like Sister Young and Brother Ben, they all possess the spirit of the Lord, and their lives have been blessed because of it. They have faced some devastating blows along the way. Some people may have given up, but not these six soldiers. Sister Young taught them better than that. Through the good, the bad, and the ugly, the Young family stands strong in the Lord.

In the end, on May 18, 1988, Sister Linnie Thomas Young passed away from death to eternal life. Some may say she died too soon, but we know that all things work together for the good of those who love the Lord. We know that all things happen for a reason. God sent Sister Young to complete a mission. Whenever God sees fit to call one of His soldiers home, I'm sure we all agree that He reserves the right.

> *"...the LORD GAVE, AND THE LORD*
> *HATH TAKEN AWAY; BLESSED BE THE*
> *NAME OF THE LORD." JOB 1:21B*

While Sister Young lived, she honored God in all that she did. Sister Young lived a selfless life. She was a true servant. In humility, she found joy in being the wind beneath the wings of so many. Putting the needs and dreams of others before her own was how she loved you. Just as Christ put aside His life for the world, Sister Young walked in that same effort and, because of it, many people will never forget her love.

**"Greater love has no one than this, than to lay down one's life for a friend." John 15:13**

# The Legacy of Sister Young

I'm TIRED OF CELEBRATING the hoochies. That's right. We look up to professional singers and actors like their lives are the epitome of what our daughters are to look forward to. Many of them are mothers, who are involved in porn, drug abuse, multiple babies' daddies; when will it end? Instead of celebrating women of character, women of purpose, women of integrity, the world has brainwashed us to believe that such women in today's limelight are who we should strive to become. The Jezabell & Deliliah spirit still exists among us. Some mothers even teach their daughters to, *"Use what you got to get what you want."* Instead of creating a Godly sisterhood, we are carrying out a sinful "hoochiehood".

So what is the hoochiehood? It certainly is not the sisterhood that Sister Young worked so hard to create. The hoochiehood is what we see on the reality shows today. The hoochiehood exists among generation after generation of teen pregnancy. The little girl dancing nasty and talking smart, while being encouraged to do so by an adult woman, who should know better—hence the hoochiehood. The hoochiehood is unladylike, undignified, classless, and shameful. When we see the hoochiehood show her ugly face, we should be embarrassed. Our spirits should grieve. Yet, we do a double take. The stories and articles, we read. The weekly episodes, we never miss them. We let the hoochiehood entertain us and to our daughters it becomes their future. So as we celebrate this cunning, hypnotic mindset, we merely pass the baton down to the younger sisters. By our actions, our words, our music, and the things we glorify, we are keeping the "hoochiehood" alive and strong.

> *"For they mouth empty, boastful words and, by appealing to the lustful desires of the flesh, they entice people who are just escaping from those who live in error." II Peter 2:18*

Who can behold a Virtuous Woman? We have all heard about this blessed woman in the book of Proverbs. A woman like this should be celebrated. If we say "no" to this hoochiehood non-sense and "yes" to the truth, maybe one of us will be the next "Virtuous Woman." Better than that, maybe this is what we can raise our daughters to become. What more could a mother ask for? What a wonderful thought.

So, let us celebrate our modern day "Virtuous Woman" in the person of Sister Linnie Young. Let it go down in history that a woman of humble beginnings beat the odds and lived her life under the light and anointing of God. Her life story will be an inspiration to many to come. She has established the blueprint for children, college students, wives, mothers, and Christians in general. I'm not saying that we should try to duplicate her life, for that would be foolish to suggest. I am saying that we should look to her legacy for hope that if she could do it, then so can we.

Sister Young's life showed me what God desires for all of His people and that is abundant life. Her life and her soul were extremely prosperous by spiritual definition. Not to say that she did not face struggle, pain, and sorrow along the way. On the contrary, Sister Young simply handled her struggles differently than most people. Her faith was always enormously bigger than any of her problems. We allow our problems to be bigger than our faith, and that is what brings forth the stress and anxiety that we sometimes take out on our children and loved ones. Sister Young's faith, however, was powerful enough to crush stress like a little ant. She always knew that God was in control of all her problems. If her family was hungry and needed food, she looked to God. Oh wait, that reminds me of one more heart-felt story that I'd like to share. This is a prime example of how Sister Young illustrated her faith in God to handle all her problems, whether big or small.

Once the children remembered being home and there was nothing to eat in the kitchen, neither was there money to buy food. Sister Young was so in tune with God that she was led to load all the children in the car and they headed to McDonald's. Now back then, Mickey D's was a luxury, a special treat, a time of celebration. People did not eat there all the time like we do today. On any other trip to McDonald's, the family would be ecstatic, but on this particular instance, they knew they didn't have money so, why were they going? None of the children can tell you what Sister Young said to the manager. All they knew was, everyone ate good that night, free of charge. Sister Young was not the type of person who played the "pity" card, looking for a hand out. This whole situation was uncharacteristic of how she did things. Yet, instead of worrying about how her children would eat, she allowed her faith in God and her obedience to the Holy Spirit's direction to feed her children that night. She gave God her problem and looked to Him to provide the solution. And He did!

Sister Young lived a good life. She offered the joy that she had within to all people. She did not beat the gospel over your head with a stick. She wasn't too holy to laugh and have fun. She walked the straight and narrow path, with her head held high and her eye on the prize. This is why she has left such a strong legacy for us. Finally, we have someone who got it right.

Sister Young's legacy lives on through the *"Linnie Thomas Young Women's Retreat"*. What a wonderful reason for women of the U. S. to visit Memphis, TN! Acting in obedience to her spiritual call of purpose, Sister Young started this retreat back in 1980. She was led to gather together hurting women in need of hope and salvation through Christ Jesus. So, she put together a two day/one night retreat and the reception was so well received and spiritually anointed that, by popular demand, it turned into an annual event. Her desire was to direct women to earnestly and actively seek God's will for their lives. Originally, it was merely called, "Women's Retreat", but since her passing, it was renamed to the *"Linnie Thomas Young Women's Retreat."* Her three daughters are all involved in making the retreat a blessing for many women every year, as their mother would have wanted. It warms your heart to see the spirit of Sister Young live on through her children. Women, you may visit LTYWomenRetreat. org to attend. Speaking from experience, the Linnie Thomas Young Women's Retreat exudes her spirit and I am personally blessed by attending it more and more each year.

Sister Young is also remembered through the *Linnie Thomas Young Parent of the Year Award.*

This award is recognized at two different schools in Memphis, TN. This well respected honor is presented to the parent who generously gives of himself as did Sister Young. Sister Young certainly went beyond the call of duty by volunteering countless hours to these two schools when her children were students. Her outstanding involvement back then left such an impression that it became the standard by which parents are encouraged to strive toward. She certainly raised the bar for your everyday "room mother".

Consequently, at one of those schools, her dear friend Issac Hayes also left a lasting impression. After his awarding winning success as a recording artist and actor, he didn't forget to give back to his elementary school in Memphis. He gave back to the school by upgrading the entire music department. I often wonder how much of Sister Young's influence in Issac Hayes' childhood helped to shape his courage to go and do great things in life. Who knows? Her influence was definitely strong. Thankfully, he didn't forget where he came from and many elementary students to come have and will benefit from his success.

As Sister Young's spirit looks down on us, I know her children and grandchildren have made her proud. Her six children are like her, they don't half-step, either. We should strive to be a living example of God's glory the way Sister Young was. Maybe we can influence others the way Sister Young has and will continue to influence us all with her powerful legacy.

# Simmer & Cool

## Self-Assessment

***"Let a man examine himself" I Corinthians 11:28***

ALL I KNOW IS, I want to do better. Not just for my kids but for the kids in the neighborhood and the kids at church; for the kids at my children's school and the kids across town. From all the kids who have survived natural disasters to the kids that have lost everything through casualties of war. This is why the need for mothers to self-examine is great, all over the world. Aren't they just as innocent as any other child? Don't all children deserve our best?

What are we really giving them? What type of world are we creating right now? What will result from the issues we impose on our children from half-stepping mistakes? The cycle is so predictable. For example: I half-step on quality time which creates a lack of guidance for my child. Since my child has poor guidance or direction, he reaches out to the wrong source of direction, which is the unruly boy down the street. Then my son begins to portray behaviors that he learned from the unruly boy. He begins breaking rules and creating his own. Now, he's out of control and begins getting in trouble in school, which quickly leads to getting in trouble with the police. Another statistic.

Maybe it all could have been prevented if I had only taken time out to strictly spend with my child. Those are the moments I could have provided guidance to my son, which would have given him positive direction. It also would have acted as a subtle form of supervision, because if he's with me then he's not spending his time with the unruly boy down the street.

We make things more complicated than they really are. The main focus is to be the best mother I can be and doing so with the same responsibilities, the same busy schedules, the same problems, the same money that I already have. I can't wait until things change to be a better mother, I have to start now. That's just like someone saying that they have to get their life together before he starts going to church. God wants you now and He'll help you get your life together. Through your faith in Him, you'll have the strength to get your life together. If you could do it without Him, you already would have done just that, but through Christ Jesus you can find deliverance from every habit, sin, temptation, addiction, and every strong hold that so easily beset you. But God wants to say to us, *"Trust me, I got this."*

> **"Let us lay aside every weight, and the sin which doth so easily beset us." Hebrews 12:1**

Now ladies, this is the most important section of this book. This is the part of the recipe of motherhood that, if it were left out, it would ruin the whole dish. You may as well throw it all out and start over because you just wasted your time. Well, we don't want you to have just read this whole book and not be motivated to make a change. This was not for entertainment. No jokes, this is real talk. This is a real problem requiring a real effort from mothers to make a real difference in the lives of our children. For real!

So what are you really going to do? I'm asking you to take a step away from yourself and look at yourself? I'm asking you to acknowledge the successes, as well as, accept the failures. You may have lived your life just like Sister Young. Maybe you have had more victories in motherhood than she had and have never half-stepped a day of your life. If so, then take a moment to thank God for it because that is a true blessing. You should also pat yourself on the back for your obedience. It was your obedience that allowed God to bless your home as He has.

Now, if you are like me and you know you've half-stepped, I'm really talking to you. If you desire to step it up as a mother, then yes, I'm talking to you. Please don't let this just be another book that becomes the most recent subject of conversation among that intelligent group of readers these days. Just another tool used to have something to gossip about, poking fun at everyone else but yourself. No, God wants to minister to our hearts. We don't have time for games.

So, when I think about the subject matter of this book, I must ask myself, how do I half-step? When I look at that picture, I'm not proud of what I see. It's hard to admit things like this. It makes me uncomfortable and I don't want to focus on it. I don't want to acknowledge it, I just want to ignore it, stick my head in the sand and hope the problem goes away. We are all like that sometimes. Well, time is out for us to be that way about our children. We must admit to ourselves that we have half-stepped and ask God to show us the way out of this. He can and He wants to but do we?

Do we really care enough for our children that we will be willing to do whatever it takes to make ourselves better mothers? It might require sacrifice.

It might make us get up off our lazy behinds. It might make us change the way we spend our money. Do you think we can do this? It might make us become more responsible. Dern-it, it might make each of us a better person. Do you see the ripple effect, all because we decided not to half-step as mothers?

At the end of this section, you will find a self-assessment. This is where you will rate yourself on certain areas that are crucial needs of your children. You may also add to this list, additional areas if needed. If you know you are half-stepping in an area, you are to list your own personal commitments. It is very important that you write down all your half-stepping areas first, and then seek God in prayer before you list your commitments to change. The Word of God says, *"Ask and it shall be given."* It didn't say *"I'll read your mind and give it to you, you don't have to ask".* It says, *"Seek and ye shall find, knock and the door shall be opened."* These biblical phrases indicate that we must confess with our mouths what we want God to do in our lives. Before we can confess it, we must acknowledge it.

Once we acknowledge our errors, then we must ask God to show us the way. Our faith is the confirmation that He will lead us toward being better mothers; therefore, we must prepare to receive our request. Our faith that He will deliver us should show in our interactions with our children. Simply begin operating in what we want God to perform for us, proving that we believe God is able to sustain us and accepting all the changes that will come. Step out on what you believe; it's what faith really is.

We may not know how to begin having conversations with our children. The only way you have ever communicated was through fussing or the closed-end question/answer conversations like *"where are you going and when are you coming back?"* We find ourselves having these one-word answer chats with the children because they act like they don't want to be bothered and we let them act that way. Starting a real conversation may seem scary, but if you just start talking one day and begin asking them questions that require their opinion, we are really saying, *"God can help me and my child have a relationship so I'm going to begin walking in that victory, enjoying every moment."* This is how we watch God in action by stepping out there and allowing God to work His small miracles.

How can we look ourselves in the mirror and not question our *"pudding love"* for our children? When I say *"pudding love"*, I speak of the topic of this entire book in regards to the old saying, *"the proof is in the pudding"*. How can I prove my love for my child without nurturing, without guidance, without training, discipline, and affection? I'm saying, *"I love you*" without showing it. I'm not showing it because I'm not pouring any of my love into my child and believe me—my child sees and feels this. Our children expect certain things from Mama and when the child doesn't receive it, along comes the anger, rebellion, the attitude and the list goes on. Children know that talk is cheap. With that in mind, the reality of our actions and our tendencies to half-step thus exposes our real *"pudding love"*. How's your pudding tasting so far?

This self-assessment is very important in beginning our **"Don't Half-step Movement"**. It is my prayer that this will be something that every mother will want to take a few moments to review. The questions in this assessment will address the impact you are making toward your child's <u>mind, body, and soul</u>. By completing this, if nothing else, prove to yourself that you are giving your very best toward your children. On the other hand, if you have any amount of doubt that you are half-stepping toward your child, I strongly urge you to complete the self-assessment and immediately begin your "motherhood make-over", if you will. Let not another day go by before you make up your mind to humble yourself and grow.

## Self-Assessment

| Nurturing | Always | Sometimes | Never |
|---|---|---|---|
| 1. Does your child seek your help and advice with emotionally hurtful matters? (Disappointments, failures, difficulties, etc.) | | | |
| 2. Do you offer your child positive words of encouragement and support? | | | |
| 3. Do you communicate problems without yelling, profanity, and criticism? | | | |
| 4. Do you serve healthy foods and promote healthy eating habits? | | | |
| 5. Do you encourage and assist in achieving a healthy lifestyle? | | | |
| 6. Do you cultivate your child's spiritual growth? | | | |
| 7. Do you have personal time of prayer and scripture reading with your child? | | | |
| Comments: | | | |

| Guidance | Always | Sometimes | Never |
|---|---|---|---|
| Does your child make decisions based on your one-on-one teachings? | | | |
| Do you help your child decide on entertainment, fashion, how to spend leisure time, etc.? | | | |
| Do you motivate and push your child to strive higher and expect the best in themselves? | | | |
| Do you intervene when you see your child developing bad habits? | | | |
| Do you take a blind eye to your child's interest/involvement in smoking, drinking, or drug use? | | | |
| Do you invest time in bonding with your child to influence his/her choices and outlook on life? | | | |
| Do you minister to your child? | | | |
| Comments: | | | |

| Training | Always | Sometimes | Never |
|---|---|---|---|
| Do you personally teach your child all things you expect them to know? (Evangelism, life lessons, manners, common sense, study skills, etc.) | | | |
| Do you encourage your child to figure things out on his/her own and offer support in the end? | | | |
| Do you explain the reason behind rules in terms a child can understand? | | | |
| Do you require exercise, strenuous household chores, involvement in sports or outdoor play? | | | |
| Do you teach them how to study the Bible? (Learning the books of the Bible, use of concordance, commentaries, etc.) | | | |
| Do you minister to your child? | | | |
| Do you require your child to memorize scriptures? | | | |
| Do you allow your child to lead the family prayers? | | | |
| Comments: | | | |
| | | | |
| | | | |
| | | | |

| Discipline | Always | Sometimes | Never |
|---|---|---|---|
| Do you establish and enforce rules with consequences for violations? | | | |
| Do you regulate things that may distract your child's attention and focus away from positive things? (Certain music, movies, websites, etc.) | | | |
| Do you teach them how to control their conduct? (Quiet time, study time, nap time, etc.) | | | |
| Do you approve your child's outing and curfews? | | | |
| Do you require that your child behaves in a manner that is in line with Christian principles? | | | |
| Do you reward good behavior and take action toward bad behavior? | | | |
| Comments: | | | |
| | | | |
| | | | |
| | | | |

| Affection | Always | Sometimes | Never |
|---|---|---|---|
| Do you regularly express affection toward your child? (I LOVE YOU!) | | | |
| Do you regularly show affection toward your child? (Hugs and kisses) | | | |
| Do you allow your child, within reason, to express emotion? (Joy, sadness, excitement, disappointment, etc.) | | | |
| Is your child exposed to and comfortable with physical affection? | | | |
| Does your child understand and exercise in praise and worship? | | | |
| Comments: | | | |
| | | | |
| | | | |

| Love | Always | Sometimes | Never |
|---|---|---|---|
| Do you regularly speak and show your sincerest love for our child? | | | |
| Do you encourage, motivate and support your child in every way that is needed? | | | |
| Do you make personal sacrifices for your child? | | | |
| Do you put your child's interests as high priority? | | | |
| Do you ensure that you make time in your busy schedule to spend quality time with your child? | | | |
| Do you regularly pray for and with your child? | | | |
| Comments: | | | |
| | | | |
| | | | |

## A *"Don't Half-step"* Lifestyle
### Half-stepping Areas
(List how you have half-stepped in the past.)

Nurturing

_____

_____

Guidance

_____

_____

Training

_____

_____

Discipline

_____

_____

Affection

_____

_____

Love

_____

_____

## Strategy to not Half-step
### (List specific things your plan to do.)

Sunday

_____

_____

Monday

_____

_____

Tuesday

_____

_____

Wednesday

_____

_____

Thursday

_____

_____

Friday

_____

_____

Saturday

_____

_____

Well, you did it. No, you won't find a scoring system to tell you that you are a good or bad mother. This is only designed to give you a visual of your personal areas of development. There it is, on black and white, uncut and uncensored. It is undeniable that when your thoughts have been transferred to paper that things are perceived a little bit clearer. You have completed this self-assessment and you now have a general knowledge of what you have given less attention toward. In other words, you may have half-stepped yesterday, but today is a new day!

### *"Forgetting what is behind and straining toward what is ahead." Philippians 3:13b*

Congratulations! Admitting a problem is the first step. Anyone can take this assessment and lie on every question. However, if you are honest with yourself and decide you do want to do more in the life of your child, then you can use this to measure your weaknesses and ask God to help you not to half-step. Now you know your challenge so begin to create your strategy as God leads.

Now remember, old habits are hard to break. It's hard to teach an old dog new tricks. I could go on and on with clichés about how hard this may seem at first. Plus, the enemy does not want you to save your family so he will be busy. Just don't give up. Each victory will help you. Just remember to pray daily. God sees the heart of His people and He will be a present help when you need it. We can do this, mothers, we can.

*"I was formerly a blasphemer, a persecutor, and an insolent man; but I obtained mercy because I did it ignorantly in unbelief." I Timothy 1:13*

# Bless the Food

## *Corporate Prayer for Mothers*

WE SHOULD FIRST TAKE our children in our arms and cry a sorrowful plea of forgiveness for our half-stepping ways. If a person is truly sorry about something, they will do anything possible not to repeat the same situation. Since we know that old habits are hard to break, it's hard for a mother to change a certain practice or ritual that could date back to their own childhood experience. If a mother has never had a conversation with her child other than fussing and yelling or giving orders, then it will be a huge mountain to climb to begin intimate talks with her child. The mother may even be the youth leader of her church, but to ask her own child, "How was your day?" may seem close to impossible, at first. There are some mothers who know they should pray with their children, but to avoid rejection, they simply don't bother.

A door that you have not opened in a long time may be hard to open. You may push hard, time after time, and never get it to budge. However, if you ask for God's power and push hard enough, it will open. After you open it once, the more you open it, the easier it will become. Whether it's hugging your children or giving them words of encouragement, it may be easier said than done. The key is making a change in your own heart.

### *Create in me a clean heart, O God; and renew a right spirit within me. Psalm 51:10*

Well, after reading this book, after learning from the examples that Sister Young left us, and even after completing the self-assessment, all of this will be in vain if we don't go to the Lord for His divine assistance in correcting each of our individual short-comings. Only our Heavenly Father can tug at our hearts and inspire us to make better decisions with our children. When the old ways set in, we will be defenseless if we dare to tackle this battle alone. The enemy wants us to fail as mothers. Oh, but praise be to God that the enemy has no power over us. The devil may have his tricks, but we must be prepared to claim authority over all things in our lives that are unrighteous. The first thing we should condition ourselves to do is pray. This road will be rocky. It may even be unfamiliar to some. Nonetheless, through Christ, it is absolutely possible.

It's hard to admit to yourself that you have half-stepped as a parent. The fact is, you cannot really change your actions without changing your heart. Only God can help us with that. If we want to stop half-stepping with our children, then we must stop half-stepping with God. There is no time to waste.

So I am calling a corporate prayer for the mothers of the world. We must begin this process in prayer as God leads us through our healing, and rejoice every time we see the Lord working it out for our families. Any building must have a strong foundation to withstand the storm and the rain. There will be storms along the way for us, but we will withstand if our foundation is rooted and grounded in prayer. We must go boldly before the throne of mercy, expecting the authority of the One that keeps us from falling. So mothers, let us pray.

*"Therefore confess your sins to each other and pray for each other so that you may be healed. The prayer of a righteous person is powerful and effective." James 5:16*

# Corporate Prayer

*Dear Lord, we praise you for who you are. You are Lord of Lords, King of Kings, Lord over our souls, the very breath we breathe. Thank you for allowing us to experience another day in the land of the living. You are worthy of all praise.*

*Father, we thank you for this special gift of motherhood. Thank you for creating us to be the mothers of the world. You designed our bodies to carry your seeds as they develop inside our wounds. You gave us the strength to endure the pain of childbirth. You chose us to carry out this important task in life, to be shepherds over your baby sheep and for that we thank you.*

*It should be our honor and pleasure to rise to the occasion with willingness to be the best mothers we can be. For things that we have done contrary to your will, as mothers, we repent and ask for your forgiveness. Some things may have been done in ignorance and some in selfishness. Thank you for your grace when we know we have fallen short of your glory. Forgive us, oh Lord and please do not hold our children responsible for our foolish decisions and actions.*

*Lord, teach us how to love our children. Teach us the true meaning of the word. Lord, we desire the unconditional love that mothers should have for their children. Help us to emulate with our children the same unconditional love that you showed for us, Christ Jesus, when you died on the cross. Help us to seize this blessed opportunity to raise our children unto You and to be pleasing in Your sight. Teach us how Father, we pray.*

*Thank you for sparing the lives of our children. Keep your holy angels to shield them from danger. Cover them and protect them as only you can.*

*Father, we ask for your strength in raising our children to be happy, healthy, and holy. Show us how to nurture them in every way required and to give them the direction needed to grow and mature. Help us to train them up as they should go. Help us to offer Godly discipline and teach them self-control and good behavior. Teach us how to show and share with them affection and love. Help us to raise them up unto the Lord.*

*We desire to have a special relationship with our children that they may grow up with balance and confidence. Help us to always pray for them and with them. Help us to recognize ways to witness the gospel to them, to ensure they are taught of your goodness. Lord, You said in Isaiah 54:13, "And all thy children shall be taught of the LORD; and great shall be the peace of thy children." Reach their hearts, oh Lord, and save their souls.*

*We praise you in advance for showing each mother praying this prayer the areas where we have fallen short. Thank you for showing us how to do better and above all, thank you for saving our children and restoring the family. And finally, we thank you for Sister Young and the Godly legacy that she has left as a gift to the world.*

*In Jesus Name,*
*Amen*

# Buffet Feast

## Charge from the Author

THINKING BACK TO MY childhood, there was a poem we would recite that reads:

> *When you fall, fall on your back.*
> *For if you fall on your back, you can look up.*
> *If you can look up, you can sit up.*
> *If you can sit up, you can get up.*
> *And if you can get up, you can go up*
> *And reach greater heights.*
> *-Author unknown to me*

This simple poem always stayed with me to prepare me for the falls. There will be falls along this journey called life. As a mother, there will be times when you may have to struggle or do without or even cry. From seeing your child with health problems to watching your child slip deeper into a world that is not his own. No matter how difficult the situation may be, we are sustained. We may not understand the route, but if we trust and follow God's perfect path, we will find ourselves exactly where God wanted us to end up. God is the creator, the author and the finisher. If He wrote the road map, then we must not try to manipulate or predict the destiny when it has already been predestined?

I do not believe this situation that today's youth are in can be immediately fixed merely by our mothers stepping it up. Yes, our fathers, grandparents, uncles, aunts, neighbors and teachers play a significant role in all this. I can only speak from my personal experiences and I will tell you for a fact, not growing up with my mother made a lasting impact in my life.

There are many reasons why a mother may find herself, "missing in action" in the lives of their children. In my situation, this was something that was entirely unavoidable for my mother. Being diagnosed with Paranoia Schizophrenia, my dear mother was unable to play a healthy, active role in my life and the lives of my siblings. Nonetheless, there are mothers who are right in the homes with their children and they don't have a mental sickness to use as an excuse. Just like me, their children have a mother who is, "MIA" and it's a lonely feeling.

There were many, many nights I prayed to God for

my mother to come for me. Not because my life with my father and step-mother was abusive or neglectful. The fact was, any child being disconnected from her mother is devastating. The physical, spiritual, and emotional disconnect is what I am speaking of. Although we mothers are present physically, I am so glad that this book has evoked you to re-evaluate your spiritual and emotional presence in the lives of your children. We must realize how much mothers can influence the well-rounded outcome of our children, merely by offering love, discipline, support, and consistency.

An acronym for the word MOM is, "<u>M</u>anager <u>of</u> <u>M</u>any". This, in its simplest terms, describes how a mother is made to effortlessly handle wearing many hats. I understand in many cases, included among those hats are, "father" and, "breadwinner". Now, Sister Young had the support of her husband as both father and bread winner. This allowed Sister Young the opportunity to be and accomplish all that she did as a mother. This shows us how much the fathers are needed to make the family complete. Some might say, their family was in order as it relates to the "Papa bring home the bacon, Mama fry it up in a pan" conception. However, when the father, the head, is out of place, yes, it throws everything else off. A body needs a head to operate. Nonetheless, when mothers are forced to assume the father/ breadwinner roles, it can cause them to neglect their own role as mothers. If you look at the big picture, what are we really accomplishing? Yes, we worked two jobs to pay the bills and buy the children name brand gear, but when Mom is at work and the children come home alone with no parental supervision, what are we really jeopardizing with our children? They may be exposed to things contrary to what you want to show and teach them? What door does that open? I know, so many.

When we think about what the world accepts, it is simply too big of a risk to leave the responsibility of raising my children in anyone else's hands. It's time to say, *"My children will not be negatively affected by things I allowed them to be exposed to. These are my children and they are my total responsibility. So I'm going to act like it. I know what I have to do."*

I wish I could reach out and touch that young girl or young boy who carries that deep pain. You know the one that you can't escape. This is the pain that someone out there tries to ignore by calling it a teenage attitude problem. We often recognize the child's obsession to be grown too fast or their poor attempts to act grown, for that matter. Or maybe we are slapped with their gradual rebellion leading them to socializing with the wrong crowd. Let's be frank, there are children in pain out there stealing, fighting, lying, and much worse. Some children cut themselves. They would rather feel physical pain than to deal with their own broken hearts. There are some who are flirting with their dark, curious desires to involve themselves in extremely pervert acts. Some poor lost souls want to become murderers. I have heard about websites where so call "friends" encourage children to commit suicide. Many are succeeding.

Many signs are right in our faces. Some children's excessive seclusion or sadness, day after day, week after week, month after month, is simply a cry for help. We can't wait for another suicide. The point is, our children need our attention, our time, and our love. Not by being a mother who is, "missing in action" but, by being in their space, in their ear, and in their business.

If I could attack that terrible pain, if I could reach out to all the sweet children, I would gently put their hands in mine and squeeze. When I squeeze, I wish so badly to squeeze out all of the pain that they carry. Let me help carry this load. If only for this very moment, let me pull as much of that ugly, inexcusable poison from this dear child's existence. Let me be the mother to suffer from the stink of a nation of half-stepping mothers whose lack of commitment have been instrumental in the condition of today's children.

As I release the squeeze, I would welcome them

to embrace themselves in my arms, as I whisper to them, *"It's ok, Mama's here."* This hug represents our repentance for our many half-stepping mistakes. This hug is also a hug of safety. It is a hug of security. Like I said, *"It's ok, Mama's here. Mama will make it all better."*

Mothers, we must believe that we can make it all better. By the grace of God, I declare and decree we will. Mothers all over the world will humble themselves and self-reflect. We will not make any more excuses for our actions. We will bend over backwards to become better mothers. We will! By doing this, we will see positive changes in our own lives and the lives of our children. If the void, the pain, the sadness, the rebellion, the sin, the fear of our children is removed, as a result of mothers who have been motivated to half-step no more, then writing this book would not be in vain!

For children who grow up without their birth mother like I did, there is a special need for all the mothers of the world to stand in the gap. Thank God for my step-mother, grandmother, big sisters, church leaders and others who filled in the gap in my life. Unfortunately, there are many children out there who are not as fortunate as I was. Their souls are searching but they are coming up empty handed. Sister Young was a mother to many children. Steve Young quoted *"I had to tell my friends, she is not your Mama, she's my Mama."* He didn't understand then, but he now knows that she was only standing in the gap.

No matter how old children are or how grown they think they are, every child needs a hug from Mama. They all must have an adequate portion of nurturing, guidance, training, discipline, affection, and love. Some may need this longer than others, but at some point in their childhood development, I believe these things are essential for a healthy mental and spiritual upbringing.

Imagine our flower which was barely standing after suffering the atrocious storm. That half dead plant now needs an extra large portion of nurturing. If one did not give it the proper amount of sunlight and water needed, would it survive? The question is, how will the children survive the storm they have had to endure? If our children are forced to continue to suffer our parental storm, what type of adults will they be? Worse than that, what type of parents will they be?

So what's the solution? For the mother that does have to hold it down all by herself, and has little time to spend with the children, what's the solution? To the mother who has been so selfish for so long, thinking *"It's about her,"* what's the solution? To the mother who is highly recognized and noted in her career, and cannot let motherhood or anything else stand in the way of her upward success, what's the solution? To the mother with an addiction, what's the solution? Who really knows, only the Author and Finisher of them all, the Creator and the Ruler, Alpha and Omega, the beginning and the end can really answer this question. We can only ask Him to give us wisdom for our individual situations. In the meantime, how about we start with a few simple jesters?

# Don't Half-Step Movement

Commit to the following:

- Truly implement the thing you wrote in the self-assessment. Stick to it.
- Quality one-on-one time. This is where guidance and advice come in.
- Strict rules. Remember, we are the parent.
- Know our children's world. Get in their business.
- Offer positivity in their life. Show them good things and give them hope.
- Be a good example, the children are always watching us.
- Savor ever moment, tomorrow may never come.
- In all things, give thanks.
- Pray by day and by night, for our children and also with them.

As I come to the end of this long journey of evaluating the plight of a mother, I look back on where we started. My mind has gone all the way back to Adam and Eve. Oh, the burden she had to have felt as she bore children into this world of sorrow. Now, she is the only woman who knew the beauty of what we could have had. She experienced, first hand, the life of luxury, living in the extraordinary Garden of Eden. First of all, just imagine not having to go to work, ever. Before God's curse on man to have to work to the sweat of his brow, all we had to do was take care of the animals and get the delicious fruit from our appointed fruit trees and worship God and chill. There was no stress, or greed or competition or envy or any of the things that came from the curse of us having to work. Now, we run around in life, caught up in the game of business and enterprise. As if it really mattered. As if a person' career was the epitome of life's purpose. In some case, through one's career, they are able to carry out destiny, but there are still other cases where career can be a hindrance for destiny. I would have much rather eaten from the trees God instructed and still be living the good life. I'm just thinking about the mornings when you just don't feel like being bothered with the traffic and the co-workers and deadlines and the boss. You would love to just relax, as long as you wanted to. Imagine not having to get up and go anywhere. Wow, thanks a lot Eve.

I know Eve had to be sick over what she lost, not only for herself but, especially, for her children. What mother in her right mind wouldn't feel guilty about causing harm or danger to her own precious child? Because Eve half-stepped in her obedience to God and His law, she ruined the best of life for her children and ultimately mankind.

The curse of that same spirit is still alive today. Mothers are too embarrassed to truly evaluate themselves so they don't even address the problem. We just remain in our comfortable places, as a half-stepping mother, doing just enough to get by. Well, I say we defeat this spirit once and for all. It's time for us to stop giving life to the same spirit that is leading us to accept this mediocre standard of motherhood.

As long as we continue to half-step, we teach our daughters how to behave the same way. When they never see anything else, they don't know anything else; therefore, they don't do anything else. See, know, and do. See, know, and do. Let me say that again. When they never see anything else, they don't know anything else; therefore, they don't do anything else. Ladies, do you hear me. It's high time we begin to consistently <u>show</u> them how to love, so they will <u>know</u> how it feels to be loved, and our families will <u>grow</u> in God's love. Show, know, and grow mothers. Show, know, and grow.

So Webster and Wikipedia, you need to go ahead and give me my due props. I ain't playing; I'm for real. Go ahead and add "half-step" to the dictionary and

I'm not talking about a musical term. Yep, this word must be properly hyphenated to emphasize how one word needs the other to create its meaning.

**Half-step - v. a person's effort, enthusiasm, focus, and attention toward performing a specific act**

To half-step is just not good enough. To half-step puts a strain on everyone around. If you are going to do it, then do it right, don't half-step. Do we all understand its meaning? Well, let me make it plain, one more time.

If I am trying to climb some steps, I'm going to have to lift my leg a certain distance in order to move from the bottom to the top. If I am too lazy to lift my leg all the way, then there are no steps taken and no measurable movement made. So to define the word half-step, I must say, the word <u>half</u> indicates the measure of distance, effort, and end result. If I'm going to walk up those steps, I can't move my foot half way to the next step but all the way. Half way won't get me up those steps, you feel me?

So being a half-stepping mother just won't cut it anymore. We cannot continue to accept our own shortcomings. I'm gonna tell you why I can't remain a half-stepper. Me personally, here's the conviction I feel. You see, God showed me the errors of my ways in knowing the truth about my purpose as a mother. Yes,

I had a thriving career, not so long ago. I was so proud to be a banker. Being able to help people manage their finances was a joy to me. I was constantly learning new things and I'm proud to say I was good at my job. Even though I gained great fulfillment from being the person my banking clients could relate to and that they could count on. I used honesty and integrity when advising them on financial products, investments, and loans. My clients knew I would always offer my services to them, with a willingness to educate and effectively assist their needs, with no strings attached.

After being named top sales manager of the year, God was ready to rearrange my priorities and put my home back in order but I was afraid. How could I be like Sister Young and leave my job for my family? How could I walk away from a salary like mine? I wasn't rich but a decent, middle class salary like mine was hard to come by. Besides, my husband was trying to start his own business so until we could see an upward spiral for him, I can't be quitting my job. "No, no, that wouldn't be wise," or so I thought? The reality was, my season as a banker had come to an end, but I was too afraid to walk away.

People, do we realize what God is capable of doing if we only had a little faith? If only I had that mustard seed faith. Perhaps things would have gone differently for me. Either way, God still has the glory.

It was not my purpose in life to dedicate myself to being a banker. I was a Christian and a wife and a mother, yet all I could think about were my responsibilities as Branch Manager of the bank. To make a long story short, I lost my job. God was trying to get my attention. Sometimes, God has to allow multiple trials to come, in order to get the attention of hard-headed people like me. After I lost my job, my mother became fatally ill and later passed away, my husband was in a car wreck and could have died, my son developed an infection in both his eyes, which later required multiple surgeries, and my daughter had a seizure, all of this in 2 months. It took all of that, for me to see, how important it is to put God first and certainly your family before anything else in life. The fear of losing any of my family members totally shook me up. Without putting God first, how could I have handled the sorrow that I experienced that year? It's times like these that the non-believers become trapped down that highway of depression and worry. Oh, but when you "know that you know" that you have a Father who sits on high and looks down low at all your situations, you can stand.

Trials come to make us strong. I'm proud to say that I am a little stronger now. I know what it is like to feel the pain of defeat and shame when I was fired from my job. I had to learn that my success in life came from my fulfillment of God's purpose for me and not what was written on that pink slip. I didn't see the blessing that was in store for me when I was "removed" from my career, so to speak. Yes, it was a set-up for a special blessing for me. My blessing was to be able to focus on God, my husband and my children. I would often pray for God to show me how to balance it all. He had to remove all distractions first. Who would have ever guessed that my career was the distraction? Anyway, I know from experience that if it is not in God's will, it won't work. We can try to make it work, but only what we do for Christ will last.

I'm proud to say that my faith is stronger. My faith in God's power assures me that God will rescue me from any situation, whether it is financial or in healing, or simply in grace. God has always had my back and He always will, if I diligently seek Him and believe in Him. My belief that God will heal my son's eyes from Chronic Uveitis is where I find comfort. My faith is what I have shown my son and now his own faith leads him to expect complete healing. He walks in faith. No matter how hard things may be for him, he rises to the occasion. He may be visually impaired in one eye and legally blind in the other eye, but he still takes advance classes and makes the honor roll. He still plays basketball and does everything all the other children do. He makes me so proud to be him mother and so inspired to be as great as he is. His name is Skylan. We named him that because in the beginning, God created the heavens, (Sky) and the earth, (Land). If God created Skylan, He can certainly heal him. Hallelujah!

When my husband had that car wreck and his work truck flipped five times, I felt helpless and afraid. When my daughter had a Salated Seizure brought on by fever, it was also frightening. When my mother developed breast cancer that spread throughout her entire body, I didn't know what to do. The only place I could turn was to God. Knowing the prayer warriors were on post was comforting. I had a strong defense mechanism on my side. These are things that only believers can understand.

God designed us women to be strong. We have to hold it all together for our men and our children. Women have to keep it all together in most cases. We especially can't let our children see us falling apart. Who will comfort them? We have to, right? Therefore, we must be rooted and grounded ourselves. A life devoted to Christ will never, ever fail you. It will only bring all the pieces of your puzzle together. Our first step in truly being better mothers is being better followers of Christ. The secret is out. Now we know better and we must do better. We must be about our Father's business.

Call me naïve, but I do believe if we all implement these best practices that we have written in the self-assessment portion of this book, we will see a difference in the behaviors of our children. We have to save them from themselves, which is a future of more half-stepping mothers. We have to take a stand and make a difference. The first step, we have to be obedient to God. The phrase is, "show and prove" not talk and prove. Who are we to tell our children to do right when all they see us doing is wrong? They learn to love what we love and if you do it, you love it. The question is—what do you really love? Be honest.

So if there are any mothers out there who have tried to raise your children the best way you know how, but you have not invited God into the equation, I strongly urge you to start this "Don't Half-step Movement" on the right foot—by asking God into your life. How do we get to God the Father? The answer is found in John 14:6.

> *"Jesus answered, "I am the way and the truth and the life. No one comes to the Father except through me." John 14:6*

So if you believe that God sent His only Son to

sacrifice His life for your sins, then read this scripture and pray this prayer with me:

*"If you declare with your mouth, "Jesus is Lord," and believe in your heart that God raised him from the dead, you will be saved. [10] For it is with your heart that you believe and are justified, and it is with your mouth that you profess your faith and are saved." Romans 10:9-10*

**Prayer:** *Father, I confess that I am a sinner. I repent of my sins. I accept Jesus as my Lord and Savior. Come into my heart and change me. Forgive me of my sins and save my soul. In Jesus Name, Amen.*

Congratulations! Accepting Christ is the first step in becoming a better person in general, not to mention a better mother. As we stated in the beginning of the book, Sister Young's devotion to God is what enabled her to be the mother that she was. Now, if we truly devote our lives to God, He will lead us to be better mothers, as well.

We are now at the end of this recipe for motherhood and it's time to eat. We followed all the recipe instructions and we've blessed the food. The spread looks delicious and we've all found a seat at the table. It is now time to "pig out". My meaning is simple, no more half-stepping, it's time to do it right. Through God's grace, we can. We can restore that which is broken. Take back that which was lost. Be a real mother to our children. Raise them to make us all proud.

So let's reclaim what is ours. Let us unite, stand up and be heard. We are in this together, mothers. Young, old, black, white, the rich and the poor, we are all in this together. Sister Young has shown us her prize through her children. Now, let's capture each of ours. Let's all take this big step to restore the lives and future of our children, one family at a time. We have put the past behind us. We have asked for forgiveness. We have made our minds up. We will not half-step. By the grace of God, we will not half-step anymore!

*"And Jesus said unto her, Neither do I condemn thee: go, and sin no more." John 8:11b*

# Acknowledgements

I WOULD FIRST AND foremost like to thank God for choosing me to deliver this important message to mothers. As unworthy as I may be, I count it a privilege to be used by God and I give all creative accolades to the Lord for guiding my pen and inspiring my mind and heart to exercise this gift of writing. I thank my loving husband, Dale Stephens, for his support, your graphic designs, and for all the countless conversations that we had about his memories of Sister Young. I thank my children for inspiring me to always strive toward being a better mother. All that I do, I do for you: Dale, Skylan, Joyner, London, and Halana (Lani). I love you dearly.

To the Young family: Joy (Hollis), Steven (Tamara), Kevin, Corey (Tomorra), Kia (Corey), and Camille, thank you so much for allowing your mother's legacy to reach the masses. Thank you, Uncle Sonnie, for your dear stories of your sister. I acknowledge my parents, James (Sr.) and Mary DeBerry for all your support and also my siblings, Darryl Samuels (Darlette), Sylvia Knox (Milton), Donna DeBerry, James DeBerry, Jr. (Donna), Sarita Davis, Roy Davis and Angelita Eldridge. I love each of you.

Special thanks to all who shared your memories of Sister Young in great detail: Ruby Jackson, Thelma Nelms, Franco Taylor, and the Stephens family, (Dale, Peggy, Chris, and Hope.) Thanks to Dr. Ellena Gooch Reid for writing the Foreward and for speaking a prophetic word into my life – Zephaniah 3:16. Thanks to the best publicist a first time author could ask for. Irene Ford, your support was just what I needed all along. Thank you sister. I want to thank Amber Thompson and Jackie Graham for your promotional advice and thank you Bethelyn Henderson, my lovely First-Lady, for writing a book review. Thanks to my editing team: Crystal Oliver, Zara D. James, Bethelyn Henderson, Mattie D. Smith, Dr. Elisa Lima, Ameerah Harris, Camille Young, Joy Taylor, Dr. Kia Tate and Clarese Brown. Thanks for helping me dot those i's and cross those t's. I couldn't have done it without each of you. Special thanks to Marqese Miller for bringing my logo imagination to reality. Last but not least, to all my closest friends from Jackson Central Merry High School, Lane College, my Sorors of Delta Sigma Theta Sorority, Inc., and those who I have met during my career, who never let me give up on this dream. Thank you: Dr. LaTorya Hicks, Marilyn Simpson, Kynesha Wallace, Odessa Manyweather, Linda Harris, Amber Thompson, Jackie Graham, LaTonya Porter, Evangelist Norvetta Hill, Yolonda Neely, Irene Ford, the "In the Pit With a Lion" small group class led by Ministers Octavius and Tara Lamar, Pastor James E. Henderson, Minister Andrew Porter, Zoe Christian Academy staff and Abundant Life Fellowship Church. A friend really does stick closer than a brother. May God bless each of you, abundantly.

# Heather DeBerry Stephens

## Bio

WIFE, MOTHER, AUTHOR, ADMINISTRATOR, fisher of men, but most of all, child of the MOST HIGH GOD, Heather DeBerry Stephens, of Memphis, TN is the loving wife of Dale L. Stephens. Thirteen years of marriage has blessed them with two sons, (Skylan and Joyner), and two daughters, (London and Halana), ages 12, 10, 7, and 2. Heather, a native of Jackson, TN, is a 1991 graduate of Jackson Central Merry High School and a 1995 graduate of Lane College. In college, she competed in several pageants on the local and state level. She was also featured in a three page modeling spread in Ebony magazine. She also studied at the University of Memphis and she is a member of Delta Sigma Theta Sorority, Inc. After graduating from Lane College, Heather began her career in retail management. After five years of the fast pace and the long hours as a store manager, Heather decided to use her managerial skills in banking. Her career as a branch manager was very rewarding for the next seven years. Heather broke company-wide sales records and was named "Top Performing Branch Manager of the Year." She was often called on to serve on committees and assist in training seminars. Her only regret was not having more time to devote to her family.

Currently, Heather's managerial skills are now utilized in a less demanding, more purposed-filled setting. She is the full-time administrator at *Abundant Life Fellowship Church*, under the auspices of Pastor James E. Henderson. It is there that her office door is a revolving threshold for people to find a listening ear and Godly advice and counsel, as she is never too busy for those who need her. Her current career has allowed her to serve as PTO President at her children's elementary school, STAR Academy College Preparatory Charter School. She travels to Nashville annually to lobby for Tennessee Charter School funding. Heather also actively participates with the Getwell Community Business Group. Heather enjoys serving on the Prayer Ministry at her church. She prays during Drive-thru Prayer, Prayer Walks in the community, she has served as prayer warrior for her church's television broadcast prayer line, and she is thankful that God has put no limits on the institution of prayer. Her most rewarding prayers are when she prays with someone new to accept Christ as Lord and Savior.

Heather has always enjoyed writing poetry, plays, skits, and speeches; yet, writing the book, *"Mama Didn't Half-step,"* has proven to be her most enjoyable piece. Heather is often called upon by friends and family to assist whenever there is a need to have something professionally written. Heather never hesitates to share her gift of writing with others because, to her, it's just plain fun.

Heather's childhood, being displaced from her own birth mother, placed a heavy passion within her heart to encourage mothers. She believes everything happens for a reason and she understands why and how the separation from her mother will now be used for good. She explains, *"It grieves me to see mothers take for granted this precious gift called motherhood. A good mother can guide her child's life in the path of success, while a half-stepping mother can stunt the growth of her child in many areas. If mothers come together, with honest dialog surrounding this subject, we can counter-attack this spiritual warfare against our children and find ourselves victorious as mothers, just as many scriptures have promised us.*

Heather desires is that her book, *"Mama Didn't Half-step,"* will spark the momentum needed to launch this DON'T HALF-STEP MOVEMENT among mothers, of all walks of life. Heather believes refraining from simple shortcomings will lead mothers toward playing a significant role in restoring the family. Heather's witty catch-phrase, *"Just don't half-step,"* is a message that she hopes will penetrate in the hearts and minds of mothers all over the world.

Recently nominated for the prestigious "Leading Ladies Awards," of 2013, which celebrates women of faith who accomplish great things within the community, Heather is humbled and inspired to continue stronger in her faith and her service. Second to living a life pleasing before God and her family, Heather's personal mission is to motivate mothers to self-reflect and recommit towards being the best mothers they can be. Heather proclaims, *"Mothers will restore families, families will restore communities, and communities will restore the world, all by the power and grace of God. In Jesus' Name, Amen."*